Farming the Inner City for Christ

The Gladys Farmer Story

Delores Freeman Cork

Kansas-Nebraska Convention of Southern Baptists

BROADMAN PRESS
NASHVILLE, TENNESSEE

© Copyright 1980 · Broadman Press.

4263-18

ISBN: 0-8054-6318-6

Dewey Decimal Classification: 266.092

Subject headings: FARMER, GLADYS / / MISSIONS, CITY / /
CHRISTIAN SOCIAL MINISTRIES

Library of Congress Catalog Card Number: 78-74914

Printed in the United States of America

*Dedicated
to
my precious daughters
Christy and Wendy
and their
wonderful Daddy
without whose
loving patience
and
frequent baby-sitting
this book could not have been written.*

The cover design was suggested by a saying of Billie Pate:

I believe in man most when I see flowers
growing in a ghetto window box.

This appears on a poster designed by Mancil Ezell, Broadman Supplies (4349–06).

Foreword

Many wonderful Christians feel great concern for the needs of the world and eagerly jump at the opportunity to help—once they know where the needs exist. Throughout these years as a missionary I've just gone out to find the needs and then hollered for help.

I know that's plainly spoken, but that's how an association wins their city to Christ. Somebody has to go find the needs, and others will lend a helping hand. That way two sides benefit—the desperate find solutions, and the Christians experience real joy.

Farming the Inner City for Christ tells the story of the first seven years of the Baptist Center in Montgomery, Alabama, in the hope that it will open the spiritual eyes and ears of Christians everywhere to the needs in their own cities as well.

The work in Montgomery is far from complete; we've barely scratched the surface. Many lives have been changed, but as long as *any* are lost, Christians haven't done enough.

Many Christians have found great joy in service as a result of their firsthand mission involvement. Oh, if only every believer would allow himself to taste this joy!

That's what it's all about—cultivating people by ministering to their desperate needs, planting the seed of the Word of God, watering and protecting young growth, and then taking part in reaping the harvest.

Pray that you will be obedient to God's command to farm your *own* city for Christ.

GLADYS FARMER, *Director*
Christian Social Ministries
Montgomery, Alabama

Preface

The attempt of Southern Baptists to share the good news of Jesus' love has caused many to recognize that there are people even in American cities who have never heard that God wants a personal relationship with them.

Conventional church programs often fail to attract scores of individuals who still need Jesus. So, in response to this need, many churches offer weekday ministries that appeal to them through helping physical and spiritual needs at the same time—just as Jesus did.

In some cases it's more desirable for an entire association of churches to cooperate in a joint effort of Christian social ministries. This expands the work to reach more people as well as providing better staff, buildings, equipment, and more volunteers for the work.

This book relates the first seven years' experience in Christian social ministries by the Montgomery Baptist Association in Montgomery, Alabama. We hope this account will help other concerned Christians to see needs in their own cities and respond to God's guidance there.

Two chapters describe the way that God prepared Missionary Gladys Farmer to rear this infant work. My intention is not to praise Gladys Farmer but to praise our wonderful God who called her into this work. He can use any of us who are willing to commit ourselves to his will to plant the seed of the gospel that his Spirit loves to mature for harvest.

God's field is the world—even our own backyards. Potential for harvest is enormous. But the challenges are great in city jungles of spiritually choking weeds. Pray for God to motivate more laborers to commit themselves to farming the inner city for Christ.

DELORES FREEMAN CORK

Contents

1
Commitment to Farming

Ten-year-old Gladys winced as the summer storm raged in the night. Rumbles of thunder threatened to shake the trees from their Georgia soil. Cornstalks bowed low. Torrents of rain beat weaker plants to the ground. Her fear was surpassed only by her feeling of helplessness.

As swords of lightning brightened her room, Gladys noticed the Bible storybook on the table beside the bed. It was purchased from a little bundle of cash found under her grandmother's pillow as typhoid fever extinguished her earthly life during World War I.

The five Farmer children took good care of their "special" book and learned its contents almost word for word. But memories of her deceased grandmother only turned her thoughts to death and dying, and that made the storm seem worse.

Gladys knew very little Scripture that she could quote for comfort and had no personal relationship with the God who could strengthen her through prayer.

Even though her parents were strong in faith, their children lacked opportunities for their own spiritual growth. In this rural community, the Corinth Baptist Church held preaching and Sunday School only once a month. And weather conditions and childhood illnesses often prevented the Farmer family from riding in their two-horse wagon to services during most of the winter. Most of Gladys' spiritual feeding came in the spring and summer—when it wasn't raining.

Mr. and Mrs. Farmer were wonderful parents and taught their children strong character, patience, morality, and personal dignity. But the storm so damaged the crop during that year that, by today's standards, they experienced a time of poverty. Through this, Gladys learned that wastefulness was wrong and that even in poverty a family can practice a wealth of love.

Once, imitating an adult neighbor, Gladys used the only bad word of her life over the temporary loss of the family water dipper. Years later she inherited a dipper that reminds her both of the discipline that she received, to prevent future use of such language, and also the sweet peace she felt after asking her parents' forgiveness.

Conversion

But even as a child Gladys knew that just "being good" wasn't enough to make her feel close to God. She felt a fear and an emptiness in her soul that didn't pass even after the storms calmed.

In fact, the solution didn't come until during a summer revival when she was thirteen. She heard Pastor Andrew Garner preach from Acts 16:31: "Believe on the Lord Jesus Christ, and thou shalt be saved."

As she heard those words the empty spot in Gladys' soul suddenly reached out for every word. For the first time, she comprehended that God wanted to have a personal relationship with her.

Rev. Garner also shared John 3:16, and the truth sank deeper.

"For God so *loved* the world . . ." Until now, Gladys had thought of God only as a superior being far away who sent storms, received souls at death, and got talked about in church. How earthshaking to comprehend that God really *loved* people and even loved her personally.

". . . that he gave his only begotten Son . . ." As the oldest child in the family, Gladys already caught the tone

(Left) Gladys Farmer holding a younger sister, Ruth, named after one of Gladys' favorite Bible characters (Right) Graduation at last! Miss Farmer completed her seminary training at the WMU Training School, which was part of The Southern Baptist Theological Seminary in Louisville, Kentucky.

Even as a student at Tift College, Gladys Farmer sought out children to teach about Jesus.

of sadness with which her parents spoke of their baby just younger than herself who had died of pneumonia. So she knew that it must have made God very sad when Jesus, his only Son, died on the cross. ". . . that whosoever believeth in him should not perish, but have everlasting life." Just as she read this, she heard Rev. Garner explain that "to believe" meant to *receive* Jesus into your heart and life. And that's what Gladys did. She prayed for Jesus to forgive her sins and be her personal Savior. He immediately fulfilled both desires.

As the congregation sang "Lord, I'm Coming Home" Gladys walked down the aisle and told her pastor that she had just accepted Jesus as her personal Savior.

As Rev. Garner prayed with Gladys, tremendous joy flooded her soul. She knew from that very moment that she belonged to the Lord and wanted to live the rest of her life pleasing him.

After this experience Gladys looked at everything differently. She read her Bible as much as possible and tried hard to please her parents. When school started back she earned the best possible grades.

But the greatest change became obvious as the shy, soft-spoken redhead began to unashamedly share with family and friends the love of God that overflowed from her heart.

After her first experience of leading a lost friend to accept Christ, she joyfully exclaimed, "O Lord, if leading people to you brings this much joy, I want to do it the rest of my life." She discovered that the second greatest thrill after her own salvation was to lead someone else to Christ.

Commitment

In her late teens, Gladys believed that God was calling her into full-time Christian service. By this time her parents had bought a home in Waco, Georgia, and one preacher had mentioned the possibility of Gladys' becoming a missionary. But when he moved, leaving unpaid debts behind,

Gladys wondered whether she was feeling a *human* or *divine* call to missions.

She prayed for God to speak to her so that she would know for sure. There were no GAs or Acteens (then YWAs) in her church, so she searched the dictionary for the meaning of "missionary." But to "propagate the gospel" was not clear enough!

As Gladys waited before the Lord, he had a better way to give her the assurance she cried out for. From a secular magazine, in the quiet of her home, she read the story of Pearl Buck's parents serving in China. This sounded so real, so exciting, so hard, so challenging, that Gladys finally knew that the call to her life was not human but divine. When she shared her call with her family, they received it with mixed emotions, especially her mother.

But after telling them, she rushed to kneel behind her father's car shelter and prayed: "O Lord, I know little about missions; but here is my life. Take it and use it. In Jesus' name, amen." From that simple commitment, although Gladys had never seen a missionary, she rose destined of the Lord to become one!

Because this new commitment to missions was influenced by that magazine article, Gladys assumed that God would probably open a door for her in China. So she started reading everything she could get her hands on about China, beginning with Pearl Buck's book *The Good Earth.*

Everything she learned about China seemed exotic and exciting. Yet an awesome humility overwhelmed her when she thought about the honor of serving God Almighty *anywhere,* sowing seeds of the gospel to people that he loved enough to die for.

Some people expected that Gladys would change her mind about missions the way many idealistic young people do after a few years have passed. Her mother would have preferred to see her marry and settle closer to home. But God had other plans.

Appointment as a missionary requires a good education, and that costs money. During the depression her family felt fortunate to have even the necessities of life. A college education sounded like an impossible luxury.

But where God guides, he provides—even though he does so by his own timing and not always by our expectations.

It wasn't always easy, but Gladys learned patience in waiting on God. And she never stopped believing that he would work everything out for her to enter foreign missions.

For almost three years after Gladys' graduation from high school, she was asked to stay at home with the younger children so that her mother could continue working at the Sewell Manufacturing Company, making men's suits.

Since Gladys was strong in her desire for education, she and her mother then swapped responsibilities. Her mother stayed at home and let Gladys work seven more years in the same factory in order to earn her finances for college.

During all this time her mother felt uneasy about Gladys' going so far from home and often said so. Consequently, for seven years Gladys prayed for God to send her a husband, thinking that perhaps her mother would approve more if she went with a man. Yet she personally didn't care which way God chose to answer. She just wanted to get on with what God had called her to do.

But God chose to say no this time. He saw her future schedule and the unique situations in which he could use her as a single missionary.

During the years that Gladys worked in the manufacturing company, God continued to prepare her for mission service in more ways than she realized at the time.

As a seamstress she developed excellent skills that have touched more lives than she can recall. Wherever she has served, mothers have always appreciated knowing how to save money by making garments themselves or by repairing old ones to last longer.

During her spare time after work she also learned to

make lovely, intricate quilts. As a result of this skill, many people have been warmed because she also taught them to make warm covers from scraps. Missions requires many different skills to meet many different needs.

Gladys rode to work each day with her father, who was the county road superintendent for Haralson County, Georgia. But his job required him to work later than Gladys' shift, so she used even her spare time of waiting to learn many things that could be used later on the mission field. She took lessons in piano, theory, and composition and increased her savings by teaching some beginning piano pupils herself. Through the years her music has been another tool for doing God's work.

During this time she also won a radio-advertised expense-paid trip to a Stamps Baxter workshop in Dallas, Texas. The words that Gladys used to complete the winning entry were almost prophetic of what her life would later include: "I would like to be a gospel singer because . . . I feel impressed to work and sing for my Redeemer. I yearn to sing peace to the sinner, rest to the weary ones, comfort to the bereaved, cheer to shut-ins, and joy to the aged. Singing would enable me to serve better my neighbor, country, church, and God."

During this workshop, for the first time she also heard Scriptures related to tithing. After asking God's forgiveness for her sin of omission, she started a habit of tithing and giving that has multiplied blessings in her own life ever since.

God knew that missionaries often need business experience too, so he opened an opportunity for Gladys to work in the Holland Drygood Department Store during thirty minutes of her lunch hour and the afternoons when she was not scheduled for music lessons. Whether the purpose was learning skills or saving for an education in missions, this tenacious committed Christian knew that when it's God's will, there's a way!

After seven years of working and saving, Gladys turned in her resignation to Sewell Manufacturing Company so she could go to college. During that last week at work, Mr. Sewell, the owner, called her into his office. *Oh, no,* she thought, *were the sample suits I sewed for the salesmen to display all wrong?*

After entering his office, Mr. Sewell asked Gladys to have a seat. And he continued, "I see on your resignation form that you are leaving in order to study to become a missionary. So I've called you in to offer you financial help for getting through college."

Gladys could hardly speak. Her family had taught her to work for everything she got. Receiving such a gift as Mr. Sewell offered conflicted with her sense of pride. She was so astounded that it was difficult to express adequate appreciation.

Through this, God had to teach her humility in order for him to bless Mr. Sewell with the joy of sharing. And even though Gladys thought she had enough money saved for college, God knew better. Truly the Holy Spirit had motivated Mr. Sewell's generosity, and the same God will provide his reward.

Education

Ultimately Gladys entered Tift College at Forsyth, Georgia. Reverend Steadham, the pastor of Bremen First Baptist Church, recommended it as he counseled with Gladys about her education for missions. He had a daughter who was a student there, and they both were very helpful in making many meaningful contacts for Gladys.

Such a long absence from school made her feel a little rusty, but she had total confidence that, even after ten years of waiting, God would still someday use her in missions. She prayed and studied with all her might and God rewarded those efforts with good grades.

While in college she led a Sunbeam Band (a children's

mission group) in a local black church. She also grew to appreciate the importance of personal prayer and Bible study. One of her Waco pastors, Reverend Lassiter, gave her a plan for reading the Bible through in a year—three chapters daily and five on Sunday.

This approach has helped her read straight through the Bible twenty-three times. Of course, this is in addition to much topical Bible study and random reading; she always wants more and regrets that her schedule allows so "little." "After a busy twelve- to eighteen-hour day, now I tend to fall asleep after only one or two chapters a day with the Bible still in my lap," she says.

During ten weeks of the summer between college and seminary, Gladys went to serve as a summer missionary in Washington, D.C. She lived in the home of Miss Lamar Well, who was also a student missionary, and their friendship has lasted to this day. Through summer missions they helped with visitation that opened mission Vacation Bible Schools in three churches.

The Covenant Mission was started then and has since become a very large church. And the other sponsoring churches followed up on those mission Vacation Bible Schools and organized Suitland and Silver Spring Baptist churches in Maryland.

Walking the streets of Washington, D.C. was probably Gladys' first real experience with city life. Here she saw her first alcoholic, her first ghetto, and some attitudes that made city life seem like another world compared to rural Georgia.

In metropolitan Washington, this young missionary learned that reaping a harvest for the Lord requires a lot of cultivation, repeatedly sowing the seed, watering young growth with Bible study, and protecting the spiritual plants from the ever-present choking weeds of Satan.

More than ever, this on-the-field experience opened her eyes to the vast assortment of human needs and reconfirmed to Gladys that God had truly called her into missions.

So she went on to further study at the WMU Training School, which was then a part of Southern Seminary at Louisville, Kentucky. She majored in missions but took every course available in social work.

She enjoyed studying, but her first love was and is personally sharing Jesus with people. One seminary professor assigned her to work with people in the low-income riverfront community through one of the neighborhood churches.

To her surprise, those summer mission experiences in Washington had not prepared her for this at all. Third- and fourth-grade boys went wild, jumping on tables, throwing chairs, and tearing up everything in sight. The gracious, soft-spoken, and bewildered missionary hopelessly floundered in all attempts to get their attention. It was mass pandemonium.

The room in the large old house where they met looked like something from a darkened castle. The children delighted in swinging their feet outside the unscreened windows and yelling at the top of their lungs. Gladys expected one to plunge to the ground any minute. But they ignored her plea for calm.

How will I ever be able to teach God's love amid this bedlam? she wondered. The sweet-spirited and polite missionary suddenly realized what a vast gulf of knowledge lies between the textbook and practical experience.

Despite her fears for their safety, she tried every technique she knew to offer an interesting program of activities, praying that something would spark their interest enough for them to listen. The pastor of the sponsoring church felt so burdened for the whole community that he kept wanting to bring more children in. But at the moment Gladys didn't see how they could control the ones they already had.

Early in her efforts there, a professor came on a surprise

visit to observe the way she conducted her project. Gladys' heart sank. She felt confident this one observation would assure her of failing the course, prevent her graduation, and banish all hopes of an assignment to foreign missions. But instead, the sympathetic teacher saw her needs and offered a few more suggestions she could try.

As never before, Gladys now comprehended that all service requires total dependence upon God. Without his guidance we will fail.

In utter helplessness she prayed throughout the day for solutions for every tiny detail. For extra strength she disciplined herself to rise daily before daybreak and sneak away to Angel's Attic, the prayer room high in their dormitory, to get God's perspective on things before she did anything else.

She prayed daily for each child and the homes they represented. She prayed for this burdened pastor who loved these people so. And she begged for God to help her to grow in love for these who were so difficult to reach. Gradually she started seeing some results.

Any service for the Lord demands a strong personal prayer life. Prayer moves the mighty arm of God. Doubts, discouragements, and overwhelming obstacles can dissolve in quiet meditation. But without this spiritual solvent, negatives can weaken even the most well-intentioned servant who fails to spend enough time in consultation with the Lord.

Before graduation from college God answered another prayer for Gladys when the Foreign Mission Board wrote to ask if she would consider accepting an assignment to the Hawaiian Islands. War had closed the door to missionaries in China, but missions in Hawaii would still involve work primarily with Orientals.

Gladys was elated! Waiting that last couple of years seemed harder than waiting all of the years she endured since her original commitment in rural Georgia.

Sometime during those last few months of seminary, Missionary Gladys Keith spoke to a student assembly about work in New Orleans. Her experienced accounts of the needs of sin-laden lives made tears roll down Gladys Farmer's face. "How mild the riverfront project in Louisville is compared to the needs of New Orleans!" she exclaimed.

But by now Miss Farmer had already agreed to serve in Hawaii. Anyway, after the frustrations she had already experienced, she doubted that she could ever work in the situations that Gladys Keith described. So she just prayed for the people and the workers God saw both in Louisville and New Orleans and thanked God for his grace in sending her to an island in the Pacific.

Love at Enoree

During the spring of 1948, as Gladys was about to graduate, Enoree Baptist Church in South Carolina called Rev. Lewis McGaha to his first full-time pastorate. Reverend McGaha enthusiastically supported missions and encouraged his small congregation in this modest little textile community to share with the Foreign Mission Board the partial support of one missionary to the foreign field.

He first wrote asking for the name of a new appointee from South Carolina. Since none was available, the Foreign Mission Board asked if the church at Enoree would like to sponsor Gladys Farmer from Waco, Georgia.

The church voted their acceptance and wrote her of their decision. Reverend McGaha left the following week to attend the Southern Baptist Convention, not knowing she would also attend.

But our God, who often supplies unexpected blessings, caused Reverend McGaha to meet Gladys Farmer at that Convention. They talked that night and then more at length the next day of all that they wanted to do together with the church at Enoree for the people of Hawaii.

A few weeks before she sailed for Hawaii, she came to

spend time with them, visiting, fellowshipping, and speaking about sowing the seed of the gospel both at Enoree and around the world.

Not only the people of the church but the whole town fell deeply in love with Gladys. Reverend McGaha preached the Sunday morning she was there and promoted her speaking that night. The people returned and brought others with them.

Reverend McGaha recalls that service: "The house was packed that night. She held the congregation in her hand. At times there was scarcely a dry eye in the church. She had such respect for God's men of the cloth that she would not stand behind the pulpit but stood over to the side and melted right into the hearts of all the people."

The WMU, led by Mrs. Hall Fleming, sponsored a shower for Gladys and gave her an abundance of supplies to carry to the mission field that would now be worth nearly $10,000 with today's inflation. The love of this small church of Enoree offers a beautiful example of what happens when a congregation is truly motivated by the love of God.

Reverend McGaha and his wife took Gladys and the missions gifts back to Waco so that she could prepare to leave. Through the years a strong relationship with what is now called the First Baptist Church of Enoree encouraged Gladys through many dark days; and she too, by the power of God, has blessed that congregation in countless other ways.

The influence of Gladys Farmer's total commitment and dedication also had a personal impact on the continued ministry of Reverend McGaha. During succeeding years this spiritual giant in faith has led several different pastorates to help the Foreign Mission Board support a total of fifteen missionaries all over the world because through this first experience he learned how to appreciate the beauty of a truly committed life and the harvest it can produce.

Thus, even countries that Gladys Farmer never saw personally have benefited from her exemplary commitment to the Lord Jesus Christ and his leadership in the life of Lewis McGaha.

Bon Voyage

The day she had waited, worked, studied, and prayed for finally dawned. The word *excitement* fails to adequately describe the kaleidoscope of emotions that Gladys Farmer felt as she awoke, knowing that today she would at last leave for Hawaii and the mission of serving and sharing her Lord.

Everyone scurried with the last-minute packing, dreading to say good-bye.

Then with emotions too deep for words her mother said she couldn't let Gladys go.

Gladys had heard this often on weekends when she came home from college. But this time she knew her mother really meant it; and she was just minutes away from catching the train! What could she do?

The enormous love among the Farmer family restrained Mrs. Farmer from allowing her firstborn to go so far away to conditions that the war in China seriously jeopardized, even if Gladys was thirty-two years old!

Yet it was the same great love that intensified Gladys' hurt. She wanted to leave with her family's approval and best wishes. She loved her mother so much that it hurt deeply to choose between disappointing her or obeying God.

Time was running out, and Gladys' father impatiently called her to the car. She continued to beg her mother to please understand and be happy that God had supplied this wonderful opportunity. But her mother's grief closed out all words of persuasion.

Finally Gladys' father had to insist that they leave. The train had already left Waco, and he had to race to the next town for Gladys to even catch the train at all.

As they drove away, Mr. Farmer tried to assure Gladys

that he would do all he could to help her mother understand and to comfort her.

But at this moment she couldn't foresee the good relationship that would come with her mother fifteen years in the future. Right now it just hurt beyond words to leave unreconciled with one she loved so much in order to serve the One who loved her more.

2
Gaining Experience

As towering volcanic peaks, flower-laden jungles, and sun-drenched beaches edging the turquoise waters came into view, Gladys Farmer and her friend Earlene Paulk knew immediately why the Hawaiian Islands bore the nickname "Paradise of the Pacific."

Earlene was from Ramar, Alabama. She and Gladys had studied together in seminary, were appointed together, and sailed together from the West Coast to Honolulu to receive more specific assignments regarding which island they would serve as missionaries. Earlene was asked to remain in Honolulu, and Gladys was sent to serve with Dr. and Mrs. Carter Morgan on the island of Kauai. They had come to Honolulu to meet her and took her back to the small island by plane.

After landing on Kauai, Gladys discovered that the people were just as beautiful as their homeland. Their gracious Oriental courtesy and cleanliness equaled their dedicated love of family and unquenchable thirst for education.

The contrast with the slums of Washington and Louisville, where she had already served for short times, made Hawaii look almost like heaven. The Foreign Mission Board provided her excellent housing on the first level of a two-story dwelling with the Morgans residing upstairs.

In the following days they enriched her life immensely with their friendship and shared their vast knowledge of the Bible with her as well as with the people, many of whom were of Japanese descent. Work among these primarily Buddhist people frequently aroused theological questions for which Miss Farmer sought Dr. Morgan's knowledge.

This pastor of the Waimea Baptist Church had grown up in China and excelled as a scholar of both the Scriptures and Oriental customs. Miss Farmer says he taught her techniques valuable in applying the Scriptures to real-life needs and daily living; she still uses them in both witnessing and teaching.

Mrs. Morgan and Miss Farmer worked more with the women, children, and teenagers. Among other things, they visited from door to door inviting children to attend the Sunbeam Band (now referred to as Mission Friends) or the Bible clubs they held after school.

Many of the parents who were invited to church services courteously replied "Yes, yes," but never came. The Buddhist religion revolves around the goal to be free from craving, suffering, and sorrow. So they take great care to speak words that please others in order to prevent the listener from suffering from a disappointing answer.

But such compassion welled inside Gladys Farmer that she did suffer with great concern for these people who were trying so hard to live good lives without personally knowing God, the source of all that's good.

Buddhist parents want their children to continue the Buddhist customs. So children who choose to accept Christ often suffer for their faith in many ways after they recognize that customs often conflict with the Bible.

They are also expected to believe in reincarnation (the theory that after death they can return either as an animal or another person). And as part of their ancestor worship, they also put food in a shrine box for deceased loved ones to "enjoy."

Sometimes Buddhist parents arranged marriages to someone their child didn't love but who had given the parents dowry money for "custom." Young people who do not continue these customs cause their parents much grief, and children feel an inner conflict because of their great love for their families.

Having come from an experience of love in conflict herself, Miss Farmer appreciated their inner struggles and prayed diligently for new believers to have the strength to lead their loved ones to Christ. Families needed not only harmony at home but also a personal peace with the only God who could bring them peace for eternity.

The island of Kauai has a mountain famous for being the wettest spot in the world. Because of the high average rainfall, many of the lower levels are prone to flooding, which causes the people to sometimes need emergency assistance through the local Red Cross.

Once when Miss Farmer mentioned Jesus' death on the cross, one child asked, "On the Red Cross?" This was the only cross she knew about. After explaining the difference, the missionary tied the two together by telling how Jesus shed his blood on the cross so his Spirit could live within us *all* the time—not just during a flood.

About one and one-half years after Miss Farmer's arrival in Waimea, heavy rains up the canyon caused a swollen river to flood the area. After contamination of local drinking water, the local Red Cross and the missionaries worked together in setting up temporary clinics and helping people clean up the debris. They all tried to drink only boiled water, but somehow Miss Farmer caught what the doctor thought was a viral infection—perhaps because she was recovering from major surgery recently done in Honolulu. Finally the island doctor insisted that she would have to return to the States in order to get well. So, too weak to object, she prepared to leave at her regular furlough time.

Leaving these people she already loved greatly saddened this missionary who had waited and worked so long and hard to get there. But since she had no alternative, she returned to the States, believing she would receive the

needed help to heal rapidly and return soon to cultivate
souls for Christ in the "Paradise of the Pacific."

Learning to Lean

In the meantime, the church in Enoree, South Carolina,
hearing why their adopted missionary was coming home,
begged her to come live among them during what they
thought would be her "last days." Gladys refused to believe
that God was finished with her yet, but she did agree to
serve in Enoree.

On her way home from the Islands, before proceeding
on to the Baptist Hospital of New Orleans, she stopped
with her traveling companion at the Southern Baptist Convention meeting that year in San Francisco.

At the display booth for home missions she inquired about
opportunities for women missionaries working with different nationalities in the United States. The personnel offered
her very little hope, saying that more men were needed
in this relatively undeveloped work.

So she left feeling that a position in a local church was
her only potential for service until she recovered enough
to return to foreign missions.

But her recovery was neither speedy nor simple. Each
time she thought she was well, a sudden hemorrhage would
prove her wrong. Recurring bouts threatened dehydration
and brought her close to death several times.

Yet the frustration and helplessness of these humiliating
recurrences taught Gladys Farmer to lean upon the Lord
as never before. She also learned during this time to em-
pathize with others in pain. God already knew that many
times in the future she would be called upon to minister
to others waiting for the return of their health.

An Enoree doctor felt that Gladys was a victim of amoebic
dysentery and recommended tests. A dear friend, Mrs. Hall
Fleming, took Gladys to a doctor in Greenville, South Carolina, who had also served as a missionary in the tropical

regions of Hawaii. He, too, recognized the symptoms, and his tests proved positive.

He explained to her that the treatment for such a disease caused a relapse immediately after each new batch of parasites hatched. He cautioned that it might take quite a while before she got completely well and that she should remain ready to seek a blood transfusion each time.

Already very weak, Gladys requested a second test because the medication sounded so hard to take. So Pastor and Mrs. McGaha carried her to Baptist Hospital in Columbia, South Carolina. Again the test for amoebic dysentery was positive and rather critically advanced. At one time Gladys had to spend four months in this hospital and then three months at a later date.

As if this were not enough, while treating her for the dysentery, doctors diagnosed symptoms of arthritis. They expressed fear that it might be rheumatoid. How exasperating for an unwell body to enslave so willing a spirit! Even when limited in body, her focus remained on the needs God showed her; and she learned to pray with the same strength she wanted to work.

By now Gladys' furlough had expired, and she was forced to accept the sad fact that her health totally prevented her from continuing in foreign missions at that time. She fought hard against the temptation to feel devastated and clenched her teeth against the subtleties of Satan, refusing to believe that God intended to use her in missions only three years.

All this time the church at Enoree strengthened her with their love. They said she could do more with a "limited body" than most people could do when perfectly well. Her example of never giving up inspired others to get busy sharing Jesus themselves—despite their lesser aches and pains.

During this same period the Enoree church, which was building a new addition, also gave 50 percent of their budget to missions—a remarkable record for any church.

Gladys often wondered why God allowed her to experience such suffering instead of returning her to foreign missions, yet she never asked him why. It was best to simply trust him.

But now she looks back to see how much good God brought from those trying times. Nothing in her earlier training had prepared her for hospital visitation as did hospitalization itself. Each time she was a patient, the Lord brought her in contact with many she could counsel with or cheer. Many psychiatric patients relaxed and confided in her because they sensed she really cared.

While Gladys stayed in New Orleans Baptist Hospital, a registered nurse with a Catholic background confided to Gladys that she did not know Christ in the way her patient did. Gladys shared the way of salvation with her, and the nurse accepted Jesus as her personal Savior. She later wrote Gladys of the joy she found in following Christ in baptism and serving him through First Baptist Church, where she became a member.

Believing that God's Word contains solutions to every human need, Gladys searched the Scriptures avidly, hoping to find his answer for her health. But for the present she didn't find cures, only more strength for patience.

She read such verses as:

• Isaiah 26:3, "Thou wilt keep him in perfect peace, whose mind is stayed on thee: because he trusteth in thee." (This helped her say "I'm in Jesus' hands—no matter what comes!")
• First Peter 1:7, "That the trial of your faith, being much more precious than of gold that perisheth, though it be tried with fire, might be found unto praise and honour and glory at the appearing of Jesus Christ."
• First Corinthians 16:13, "Watch ye, stand fast in the faith, quit you like men, be strong." (Through this she learned

to never stop trusting God, even if, like the friends of Job, people might misunderstand her suffering.)

After many different treatments and persistent recurring episodes of illness, Gladys' doctor recommended that she return to the New Orleans hospital where she received help when she first came home. So she offered her resignation to the Enoree Baptist Church and headed for New Orleans again.

Applying the Scriptures

Soon after Miss Farmer was admitted to the hospital, Reverend Squires, whom she had helped years ago as a summer missionary in Washington, D.C., came south for a hospital board meeting. And as pastors often do upon entering a hospital lobby, Reverend Squires went through the list of patients to see if they had admitted anyone he knew and happened to discover Gladys' name.

His surprise appearance in her room made Miss Farmer feel that he was sent by the Lord. They shared their experiences of the past several years. And then Gladys confided how she had prayed and searched the Scriptures for a solution to this health problem. She felt that she had been obedient to everything but James 5:14-15: "Is any sick among you? let him call for the elders of the church; and let them pray over him, anointing him with oil in the name of the Lord: And the prayer of faith shall save the sick, and the Lord shall raise him up; and if he have committed sins, they shall be forgiven him."

Even though she had never taken this Scripture so literally before—nor has she felt led to since then—during this time of desperation and searching she asked Reverend Squires if he would assist in anointing her with oil and praying to God for a cure that would enable her to serve the Lord better than she could at the present.

Reverend Squires agreed and, at Miss Farmer's request, cleared it with the chaplain to see if it violated anything within hospital policy. The chaplain not only approved but was present in joining them in prayer to ask God for her permanent cure from amoeba.

In the hours that followed, the tests and x-rays continued. But the doctors returned with the results that no trace of the parasites could be found, even though Gladys had received no medication for cure while undergoing the tests. She praised the God who produced the cure of this condition that never returned.

Yet while reviewing the data from the tests, the doctor mentioned that even though God had obviously cured Gladys of amoeba, other results indicated the early stages of some form of arthritis—just as the doctor in Columbia had discovered. But he waved it off as too early either to prove or treat and just sent her home.

So Gladys went to Quitman, Georgia, to rest and gain strength in the home of her sister, Mrs. Brantley Plymel. Gladys still lived with missions in Hawaii always in the back of her mind. However, for now, though healed from one illness, she had to live patiently awaiting the outcome of the arthritic threat.

One day as she was leaving for an interview in Florida, Dr. Martin, pastor of First Church, Quitman, came to talk with her about serving as youth director. Gladys thanked Pastor Martin and asked him for time to find God's will since she was now leaving for this interview.

Gladys went to the Florida camp which she understood was the appointed place for the interview. But the connection was never made with the person who agreed to meet her there. Gladys believed this to be of the Lord, for already she felt that God wanted her to serve in Quitman, Georgia.

While in Quitman she learned even more to appreciate the importance of church training for Christian growth. Several youth surrendered their lives at God's call, and

Young missionary Gladys Farmer showing Hawaiian children Bible-teaching pictures.

the church was led of the Lord to open a mission which today is a thriving church.

Yet during this happy and busy time arthritis became a greater threat to Gladys, and deep in her soul she knew that part of the undercurrent of frustration she was experiencing was from not yet knowing if indeed she had rheumatoid arthritis. She knew such facts would permanently close the door to foreign missions—that door which, until now, she had declared "temporarily" closed.

Her doctor in New Orleans did confirm that fact, and she wrote the Foreign Mission Board.

Now, though broken in body, Gladys was ready to come to grips with reality—not giving in to poor health but finding a new determination to serve the Lord.

She recalled the invitation the Home Mission Board had sent her only a few months after she accepted the call to lead the Quitman youth. Daily she grew more frustrated. As always, her first love was evangelism; and during this time she experienced a personally painful drought in harvesting newborn souls for Christ. To her knowledge she led only one person to Jesus as Savior in Quitman. This troubled her deeply.

Even though she felt privileged to feed and water young believers with Bible study, she thirsted to see more lost people saved. She prayed and witnessed with vigor, but without results. "Show me why, Lord," she prayed.

During the Week of Prayer for Home Missions, Miss Farmer grew so convicted that she had to leave the WMU program to someone else and drive out in the country to pray.

Through the years many answers came during such prayer-filled drives, and she had experienced peace over many matters. But this time the further she drove, the greater the conviction grew. Finally she just had to park her car in the country and get outside to kneel.

It was then that God's Holy Spirit revealed that she had

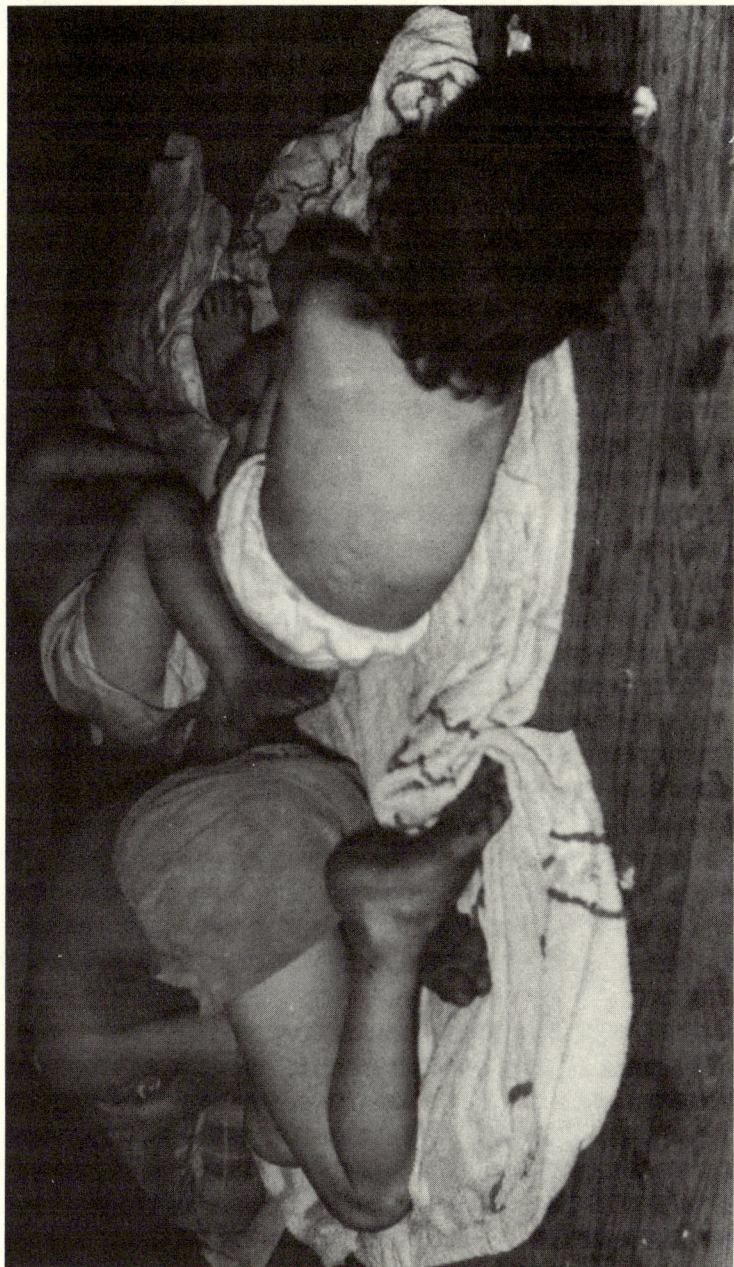

Miss Farmer made this picture at midnight without a flash. These children sleep on the porch while their mother, a prostitute, is away.

Lengthy ministry to the physical needs of this peddler and his wife awakened their spiritual appetite.

naively misunderstood that he called missionaries just to *one* location and nowhere else. In her heart she was holding out to return to Hawaii and was afraid he wouldn't use her anywhere else to his fullest potential.

Now God had to teach her that his field is the entire world and all people who live in it—even our own neighborhood. She had always assumed that church staff members and all the Christians of their congregation could take care of the United States—that missionaries should go to countries not so blessed with an abundance of churches, where there are too few preachers to share the gospel with so many. He was giving her a different work, among the downtrodden and destitute who need Jesus but who are not being reached by the average church.

"OK, Lord," she prayed. "Wherever you lead I'll go." Then a marvelous sense of relief flooded her spirit. She didn't know just where the Lord would send her, but she totally trusted him.

Restored Fellowship

With joy over the freedom of yielding to God's new directions, Miss Farmer called the Home Mission Board to see where God had prepared a need she could serve. They responded with the suggestion of either Miami or Birmingham. However, as Gladys went for her appointment, instead of either of the two cities named, she was asked to go to Columbia, South Carolina.

Humorously recalling the Louisville riverfront children, she enthusiastically accepted and trusted the Lord to supply all her needs.

Before preparing to go she told her mother of this decision. After fifteen years of cool politeness between them, she really didn't expect an excited reaction, but she was literally shocked when her mother replied, "Well, I was wondering when you would return to missions." Now Gladys wondered if her mother really agreed with her decision.

Noticing her daughter's obvious surprise, Mrs. Farmer spoke in a quiet, serious tone: "Gladys, I want to tell you something I've never told you before. When you were just a toddler, we lost your baby sister Beatrice with pneumonia. You were also very sick, and your father and I couldn't bear to think we might lose both of our babies in the same year.

"So we prayed that if the Lord would spare your life we would dedicate you to his service—but I always hoped that promise could be fulfilled at home. But when you thought God wanted you to go overseas, I just loved you too much to let you go.

"During all the pain you have suffered with the amoeba and arthritis, the Lord has dealt with me quite severely. Now I'm willing to give you up to missions, wherever he wants to use you. Yes, I gave you to the Lord long ago. Now go serve him the best way you can."

Tears of joy flowed down Gladys' face as she hugged her mother and recalled the Bible story of Hannah dedicating young Samuel.

"If only you had told me sooner, Mother," she cried. "The last fifteen years could have been so much sweeter. But thank you for telling me now."

Learning to Listen

Life in Columbia seemed again to Gladys as if she had moved to another world. The people looked different, talked differently, and acted differently from the Oriental culture of Hawaii. But after listening awhile, she discovered that they too thirsted for love and desperately needed Jesus in their lives.

It was now in the late 1950s, and Miss Farmer lived in an apartment in the largest of the three missions, called the Reece Good Will Center, with missionaries Miss Evelyn Stanford and later Mrs. Carolyn York. Living at the Good Will Center made the missionaries accessible to the people twenty-four hours a day, and Gladys loved it.

The patchwork location characterized the enormous variety of needs that existed in this melting-pot community. Residents could boast of being within a stone's throw of both the luxurious governor's mansion and Potter's Field, the burial place for the prison's unclaimed dead; of living along the dirt street that bordered the state penitentiary; and of hearing constant barking from the nearby dog pound.

The Fornance neighborhood, in which they also ministered, consisted of two-room shanties, often overflowing with children but without running water until the city forced reluctant landlords to build cold-water bathrooms between the already close together houses.

Unfortunately, the neighborhoods themselves probably influenced some of their residents to commit crimes that later put them in the nearby prison. Illiteracy, overcrowding, the often turbulent or broken homes, alcoholism, prostitution, street fighting, and theft were just a few common occurrences that everybody took for granted on Gist Street.

But, remarkably, out of this environment also came many jewels for Jesus.

The health department declared the community in the Fornance area a breeding ground for polio, whooping cough, and typhoid. The sanitation was so poor that whole families frequently required treatment for worms that even came out of their noses.

As they listened, the missionaries heard a great variety of hurts from the people and tried to help, along with many dedicated volunteers from the churches of the Fairfield Baptist Association. They varied their programs to match the needs of the people. Nurses came weekly to give immunizations upon request. Doctors came once a month to treat sick children for free.

How wonderful to see how health care has improved over the years! Mission clinics were more needed in the 1950s than now because federally funded clinics had not grown to such proportions as today; neither had the amount of welfare checks.

Eventually a dental clinic was added to the Columbia ministry. The dental association called to see if the good will center knew of people who needed work done on their teeth. Students coming into the city to pass their state board exams needed practical experience. Truly this seemed like answered prayer to many suffering from toothache pain but unable to pay a dentist.

Volunteer barbers and beauticians also offered their skills and witnessed to people while cutting their hair. Homemaking classes, lessons in literacy, tutoring for slow students, a food pantry, a clothing room, frequent use of the center's hot showers and telephone—all were combined with classes in Bible study to meet the spiritual needs of the people at the same time they helped the physical needs.

One lady who enrolled in the literacy class was so painfully shy that she withdrew from group conversations. She, like many illiterate people, felt too embarrassed to let others hear her verbal limitations.

But the love and warmth she felt among the Christians at the good will center eventually melted her defenses, and they taught her to read. After many months of cultivation, this precious lady stood before a special gathering for volunteers and the associational missions committee and read at length from God's book. Many tears of joy were shed that night by those listening.

In listening to people, Miss Farmer also heard many children and youth express embarrassment over their parents' sinful life-styles. Quite often those children lived the strongest Christian witness within their homes. Many provided their parents excellent examples of Christlike love.

One teenage boy who faithfully attended the center's boy's club and then joined the adult men's class learned to love the Lord with all his heart. But living the Christian life grew increasingly difficult in his home. His mother lived in open adultery in a house full of young children.

The occupation of her adult "boyfriend" was to go out at night to steal. On the next morning he often spread the contents of his night's work before the admiring eyes of the children.

The teenage Christian boy deplored such sins in his home and took it upon himself to teach and discipline his younger brothers and sisters about the truths of God and the difference between right and wrong.

Just before Christmas, in addition to Bible study, the men and older boys at the center made broomstick horses for "Santa" to deliver later in their homes—all but one, that is. While admiring the toys he had made, this fine young man said, "Santa Claus ain't gonna get credit for this. I want my brothers and sisters to know I made it 'cause I love 'em."

The extension ministry from the good will center helped the families of inmates in many different ways. And wives and children often mentioned those benefits as they visited their imprisoned loved ones. Eventually such respect grew both inside and outside the prison walls that inmates increasingly invited spiritual counselors to visit them in prison.

Miss Farmer tenaciously believes that *no one should be considered hopeless.* On one occasion missionaries made more than twenty visits to a home that included a mother with mental illness, a deaf child, and an alcoholic father. The family suddenly moved and the center didn't know where, but they continued to pray for them by name.

After another eighteen months, only a few days following the death of Miss Farmer's father, a knock came at the door. So many kind friends had come to express their sympathy that she thought it might be another comforter. But instead, it was the man who had turned them away from his door so many times in the past and then moved away.

He said, "I want you missionaries to know that your witness to us old bootleggers, and I'm the chief, is not wasted. All you ever said to me came back again and again. My wife died last year in the state mental hospital; but thanks to God she became a Christian just in time.

"My little girl went away to school for the deaf. I want her home this summer, but they said I have no home fit for her. I cried in the midnight hours on my knees for God to have mercy on me and forgive me—to really save me. Finally I trusted Christ and peace came, a peace I've never known before.

"That was about four months ago. I have nothing to eat; my car's gone; my clothes are worn; and I'm sick. But still I've got no desire to turn back. I want to join a Baptist church and go all the way in the Christian life."

The hearts of believers in local churches were touched to action as missionaries shared this loving parent's need. Food was provided and furniture supplied for a room where his daughter could spend her summer holidays.

The next Sunday Gladys saw her own father's suit on that converted bootlegger as he walked down the aisle of a local church, confessing Christ as his personal Savior.

From that day on he told multitudes of his friends, "Jesus the Son of the living God will give you new life too. I know. I was once a chief of bootleggers. But now I'm a child of the King."

Miss Farmer had served over eleven years in Columbia and was now on crutches, with much medical care. This was a time of testing; she longed to work freely but was too limited in body. At the request of the association she took a leave of absence to recover from a recurrence of the rheumatoid arthritis.

This resulted in a five-month sick leave and termination of her service in Columbia. But again Gladys looked unto the Lord Jesus, quietly waiting for his direction, refusing to let anything stop her from serving the Lord.

During this time she did in-depth Bible study and found refreshing new strength with her mother at her home in Albany, Georgia.

One day as Gladys prayed she picked up a road map. Where did God want her to serve? Where could she also give her mother the care she wanted to since her father's death?

Gladys prayerfully drew circles around three cities—Tallahassee, Florida, Phenix City, Alabama, and Dothan, Alabama. As she continued to wait upon her Lord, Dr. Brantley called from the Home Mission Board, saying that she would no doubt hear from Phenix City because he had given them her name.

How beautiful! It was just like God to give her a field of need with a supportive association, only ninety-two miles from her mother's home in Albany, where she could drive her back for occasional visits. And her mother spent many happy days with Gladys on this field before her death.

Gladys looks at her Phenix City experience this way: "I praise God for his divine guidance. The work was blessed of him; many were saved. Except for the challenge of opening new work in a larger city, I would have loved working with the director, Reverend and Mrs. Palmer, and the precious churches there until retirement.

"But then God called from Montgomery—just as realistically as he did from each of the other fields."

3
Purchasing the Land

"In the beginning God . . ." (Gen. 1:1).

That's how all good things start, even home missions in Montgomery, Alabama.

In the beginning God heard desperate cries for help.

In the beginning God knew only he could fill the needs.

In the beginning growing Christians looked for ways to serve.

In the beginning a man with vision led an association to establish a Christian Social Ministries.

In the beginning, and even now, God is behind it all.

Climate of the City

Perhaps an overview of the social and spiritual conditions of the city will illustrate the mission needs of Montgomery. During the turbulent '60s, the construction of two major interstates crisscrossed many inner-city homes and either forced or influenced their residents and three large churches to relocate.

The total complexion of the community changed. Instead of lifelong residents, an integrated population of usually short-term, lower-income people moved into many of these dwellings now put up for rent. While some homes suffered demolition, others were rezoned and sold as office space.

Historic preservation saved a few architectural masterpieces, but not all. Many antebellum mansions house genteel aristocrats who endure the effects of inflation on such fixed incomes that they often cannot afford expensive repairs. Swallowing their pride, many felt compelled to chop the symbols of their heritage into several different apartments, single "Rooms for Rent," or just sell it outright to a real estate company more capable of managing the headaches of rental property.

Many people from the inner-city ghettos moved into the several modern brick housing projects built by the federal government where rent is based upon income. Unfortunately, even in these satellites of the inner city, the problems remain the same because people's habits stay the same.

Unfortunately, the building of churches near these new communities hasn't kept pace with the building of these apartments. And many black people lack a convenient place of worship in surroundings that welcome their presence.

The primarily white congregations who chose to relocate left hundreds of families in the inner city with a very limited choice of Baptist churches.

Ever since the city's historic ancestors gave birth to the Confederacy, Montgomery has served as a political platform for many social issues. Rev. Martin Luther King held a pastorate only one block from the state capitol on Dexter Avenue and used its steps as a background to preach for justice for all citizens. Former Gov. George C. Wallace put Montgomery in the national spotlight repeatedly during his four attempts for the presidency and during three terms of service as governor. Such emphasis on provocative issues encourages private citizens to also define their own personal attitudes on such matters and greatly influences people's attitudes while serving in missions.

The population of this medium-sized city is comparable to Waco, Texas; Saint Cloud, Minnesota; Lynchburg, Virginia; and Tallahassee, Florida. Montgomery residents represent more than thirteen nationalities, and over one-third are black. Maxwell Air Force Base and the former Gunter Air Force Base have contributed greatly to the increase of internationals. Over seven hundred residents speak Spanish as well as English.

All of these language and cultural differences encompass many special mission needs that most local churches are seldom prepared to handle, but genuinely wish they could help meet. Thus people preparing to open new Christian social ministries depend on a total perspective of both the needs and the resources of the city.

Despite the great emphasis on education heard from the halls of the state capitol and five local colleges, over two thousand Montgomery citizens have never attended school at all; and over twelve thousand quit sometime between the first and seventh grades. Quite predictably, the resulting degree of illiteracy swells unemployment in the city's largely white-collar job market. An inability to read lessens not only their chances to find work but greatly complicates every part of their lives.

Economic inflation hurts in that one-third of the city's population live below the national poverty level. In addition to many who are disabled and retired, poverty in Montgomery engulfs more than fifteen thousand children. Regardless of the varied circumstances that produced their common plight, many of the poor feel too weighted down with daily frustrations to prepare for a brighter future and need much encouragement just to survive the present.

One-tenth of Montgomery's adults have lost their mates by death. Many others chose to divorce. Over six thousand Montgomery women are the heads of their households. Lower-paying jobs, loneliness, and the inability to cope with daily pressures overwhelm many into lives of depression.

All of these factors are typical of life in any city and produce much fertile, unclaimed land for Christians willing to farm the inner city for Christ.

Montgomery Baptists Take Action

Rev. J. Frank Hixon, director of missions for the Montgomery Baptist Association, saw all of these conditions and grew increasingly convinced that a Baptist Center could minister to such a vast variety of needs better than could the individual churches or secular social organizations.

Yet most churches get so involved in meeting the needs of their own congregation that they have little time for weekday missions—if, in fact, they truly comprehend the extreme needs.

In most American cities there are many untouched areas where souls must be cultivated with actions of love before the people would ever think of coming to church. But isolated emergency clothes closets, food pantries, and benevolence funds usually fail to witness in-depth or long enough to see real spiritual growth among the recipients.

In addition to an abundance of excellent preaching, many Montgomery churches offer kindergartens, fellowship meals, bus ministries, and Vacation Bible Schools in the summer. Choirs, Bible study, mission organizations, and recreational activities strengthen all who come. Yet most of the recipients of these services come from the same social level as those who present the service; as a result, the undeveloped areas are overlooked.

Despite such wonderful opportunities for service, many people hunger both physically and spiritually outside church doors.

Montgomery Christians recognized this and looked for ways to put feet on their faith and love. The director of missions for the Montgomery Baptist Association knew from observing the experiences of other cities that a Baptist Center would guide Christians to needs they might never know existed. In answer to many prayers, God seemed to impress upon Director Frank Hixon that the teamwork of an entire association offered the best solution for the total mission needs of Montgomery.

Acting upon what he believed was the leadership of the Lord, Reverend Hixon made the following proposal to the executive board on April 22, 1968:

"I have a matter that I want to discuss with you this morning that is possibly the most important item that I have ever brought before you. It has to do with the future of Baptist life and work here. It is, in my opinion, the most important matter to confront Montgomery Baptist Association in a decade. What I want to talk with you about is an expansion of our Baptist program here in Montgomery by adding a full-time, fully trained person to our staff to serve as Director of Christian Ministries, or some such title.

"This person would perhaps work in several areas such as Juvenile Rehabilitation, Counseling, lead in establishing neighborhood centers in the inner city, with weekday programs to nursing homes, jails, correction centers, aiding released prisoners, and also other areas . . . .

"If we have the will to do it, we can develop a program that will be increasingly important as the years pass. History and the rapidly changing city will not wait for us to hedge or delay. Some are saying it is already too late to reclaim our cities. This may be true in Baltimore, Washington, Philadelphia, or New York. But this is not true in Montgomery! If it were, we would fold our hands and wait for the worst.

"While we have an alternative, I hope that with determination and enthusiasm we will move toward adopting such a program as I have indicated. We have the capability; we have the resources; *but do we see the need?*

"What will this do for our churches? It will strengthen them. It will encourage compassion, without which our churches will die anyway. It will make Montgomery a safer, saner city. It will reach people for Christ.

"This means that we will have to rethink our mission

The first Baptist Center of Montgomery, Alabama (Photo by Roger Patton)

(Upper) Rev. J. Frank Hixon, director of missions, works with his hands as well as his heart. (Photo by Roger Patton) (Lower) Preparing the building to receive the people

planning and giving. It will mean that perhaps more of our mission money will go to the local program. It will mean that every church, suburban or otherwise, must give wholehearted support."

A discussion followed Reverend Hixon's proposal to clarify some of the details. But the pastors voted unanimously to start the committee work for this multifaceted Christian social ministries, with its headquarters to be in the Baptist Center they would organize first.

God's Choice of a Building

The choice of an adequate building and its location ranked high on the list of priorities for establishing such a ministry. It needed to be easily accessible to people without transportation and yet obvious to others not yet familiar with neighborhood streets.

When urban renewal scatters low-income residents into many isolated areas, as it has in Montgomery, a central location often becomes necessary for a ministry's success— at least until other centers can be established.

Many prayers preceded the establishment of the Baptist Center in Montgomery—prayers for God's clear revealing of the city's needs, guidance of the committees at work, the right building in the right location, and God's choice of a director. Everyone recognized the extreme importance of God's leadership if this work would lead souls to him.

While driving around the city Mr. Hixon wondered if a vacant old house would answer their needs, but none seemed just right. Then suddenly a "For Sale" sign in front of an old abandoned synagogue on the corner of High and McDonough Streets caught his eye.

This location is halfway between the governor's mansion and the state capitol, one block from the city library, within walking distance to downtown and quickly visible on a main thoroughfare. Yet it is in crime zone number 1, centrally located between many pockets of poverty, and in the section of town with the greatest percentage of elderly citizens.

After Brother Hixon parked his car and walked the grounds of the vacant synagogue, he discovered an unlocked door. So he toured the inside. Lovely stained-glass windows graced the chapel walls with scenes depicting love for God's laws. And the abundance of smaller rooms offered ample space for Bible classes.

He wasn't sure just how they could use the ceremonial showers in the basement, but use of the spacious kitchen required little Baptist imagination. The total building came closer to all that a Baptist Center would require than anyone had yet dared to pray for.

On that day and for several days thereafter, Brother Hixon tried without success to contact the real estate agent. Then Dr. White, the pastor of First Baptist Church, told him that the owners of the property belonged to his church and that he would be glad to introduce them.

After meeting Dr. and Mrs. C. B. Relfe, Brother Hixon learned the history of the lovely yellow brick synagogue. After the departure of the original Jewish congregation, a Pentecostal group and then a small private school had used its facilities. The Relfes bought the building with plans for tearing it down in order to expand their nursing home next door. But they later decided differently and were now just using the building for storage of equipment and supplies.

Dr. and Mrs. Relfe were delighted to hear that the property would be used for a Christian social ministry. Through many years of private practice and experience with the nursing home, this Christian couple had observed abundant needs among many of their indigent patients. They also appreciated the importance of teaching for the prevention of broken lives.

In addition to selling the building to the Montgomery Baptist Association at a reduced price, the Relfes served

God there for several years by giving their time, their skills, and generous gifts.

Defining Mission Goals

Director Hixon and Rev. Chester Jernigan, the moderator of the association during that time, led many meetings in order to lay important groundwork.

In addition to considerations about the building, committees also met to discuss what help secular agencies already provided and to draw up an outline detailing the purpose, goals, and programs they believed would begin to meet the needs in Montgomery.

So many mission-minded Christians have written the Montgomery Baptist Center asking how this work was organized that we share much of this information here and in other chapters in the hope that other associations might profit from these experiences.

The Special Ministries Study Committee surveyed programs of Baptist Centers in other cities and came up with the following report:

The following recommendations are based on an extensive study relative to areas of special need in the city of Montgomery. An attempt has been made to contact Service Agencies and Organizations to determine unmet needs and to interpret the concern of the churches in the Montgomery Baptist Association for developing an effective Christian ministry in the community.

These recommendations reflect the needs as determined by the Special Ministries Study Committee from the study of the community as designated by the Executive Board of the Montgomery Baptist Association.

I. Program of Cooperative Christian Ministries

Based on the unmet needs in our community, it is recommended that a Program of Cooperative Christian Ministries be established. This program would be a cooperative ministry sponsored by the Home Mission Board, the State Mission Board, and the Montgomery Baptist Association.

II. Purpose

It is recommended that the purpose of such a program would be to coordinate and to sponsor Mission Action Programs which are Christ-centered and church-related. Such a program would provide for church involvement in a vital witness and ministry through areas of unique opportunity in the community. Due to the fact that Second Baptist Church and Goode Street Baptist Church have already moved and Clayton Street is planning to move, the emphasis of this program would be an inner-city ministry attempting to meet the needs of this large vacated area.

III. Plan

In light of such a program, it is further recommended that:

1.   A Director of Cooperative Christian Ministries be secured to direct such a program.

2.   The director will be under the direction of the Association and the Superintendent of Missions.

3.   The director shall be secured with the understanding that he work toward the establishing of his work from a central location in the downtown area.

4.   The policies governing the work of the director shall be formulated by the Missions Committee of the Association.

5.   The Home Mission Board and the State Mission Board shall serve in an advisory capacity in giving guidance to the program.

6.   The Budget Committee and the Missions Committee would work out the cost of such a program in light of the help that would be given by the Home Mission Board and the State Mission Board.

IV.   Program

It is recommended that the Program of Cooperative Christian Ministries grow out of our understanding of existing needs in our community. Every strategy will be used in an effort to *communicate the message of Christ in vital and attractive ways.*

However, after looking at our needs and studying many programs from other parts of our Convention, it is recommended that we strive toward establishing a program very similar to that of the Madison Baptist Association.

It is suggested that we work toward providing six major areas of opportunity with emphasis upon the first two areas in our establishment of the program.

The areas of opportunity recommended are the following:

A. *Mission Centers*

The Director would work toward the establishment of centers in the most needed areas. Leadership for this work should come from groups within the churches of the association. The Director would work in agreement with the Missions Committee in assuming the responsibility for setting up the program of work, enlisting, training and supervising the workers from the churches. Activities would include such things as: Bible Study Classes, Club Activities (teenagers, schoolchildren, mothers, preschool children, and senior adults), Study Halls, Individual Tutoring, Recreation, Visitation, and Personal Work with families and individuals.

B. *Family Services*

One of the greatest needs in our community is juvenile rehabilitation, preventive and corrective. Other areas would be counseling, foster homes, institutional care. One of the major ministries would be that of referral to the many agencies that offer help.

C. *Friendship Program*

1. Host families for Allied Officers.

2. Host families for single men at Maxwell and Gunter Air Force Bases.

D. *Church Weekday*

Working with churches in setting up and operating ministries to the community through the local church. With the new organizational plan for the WMU, the director could help coordinate the work for the mission action groups.

E. *Exceptional Persons*

Senior citizens, illiterates, retarded, deaf, blind, etc.

F. Joint Committee

Due to the fact that much of our work will be done in communities that are predominately Negro, an attempt should be made to establish joint cooperation with the National Baptist Churches in the community. Consideration should be given to the proper way to cultivate a working relationship with these fellow Christians in working more effectively in areas of the Mission Centers.

God's Choice of a Leader

During the same time, the personnel committee met to consider potential leaders for this work and agreed that the future leader's responsibilities should include the following:

• To plan and coordinate all programs of the Christian social ministries under the supervision of the director of missions.

• To select, train, and assist enlisted personnel.

• To budget finances, answer phone calls, write letters, file reports, promote the work in printed media, and perform speaking engagements upon request.

• To participate in conventions, special studies, projects, and innumerable meetings conducted by the association, state board, and Home Mission Board, etc.

But far more responsibilities define themselves automatically through the repeated knocks on the door and the ringing of the phone. In Baptist Center work, a missionary commitment that says "Wherever He Leads I'll Go" requires one to become much more of a servant to the people than just a planner and secretary at the desk. *People* must always come before *things.*

Even the personnel committee might not even have fully comprehended such requirements, but God knew. He attracted them to the work and personality of Gladys Farmer, missionary in charge of the Baptist Center of Phenix City, Alabama, at that time.

The more they considered her experience and dedication,

the more they became impressed that the Lord was leading them to call her to start the work in Montgomery. She had supplied much helpful advice to the committees establishing this work but had no idea that they were also considering her for its leadership.

Reverend Hixon wanted to let more preachers throughout the city meet and hear Miss Farmer speak before they considered extending the call. So, without her knowledge of their intentions, he invited her to speak to a large group of pastors at an associational budget meeting. Since she certainly had experience in squeezing the most benefits possible from small budgets, she didn't suspect that her listeners were judging what she said for any other reasons.

After she finished, everyone mingled around in fellowship and came up to meet her. Then one cheerful pastor introduced himself and said to her quite openly, "Why don't you come to Montgomery?"

Miss Farmer flushed with embarrassment that anyone would misconstrue this speaking engagement as her desire to solicit such an invitation to move. She made a point of explaining her embarrassment over the preacher's statement to Brother Hixon as he took her on a tour of the state Baptist Executive Building the next day, saying that she enjoyed working in Phenix City and had long-range plans for retiring there.

She still didn't know that God planned differently. Brother Hixon then told her of his concealed intentions for inviting her to speak, how pleased they were, and that they believed her experience could be extremely valuable in starting this work.

Shortly thereafter, Montgomery Baptists voted unanimously to call Miss Gladys Farmer as director of their newly formed Christian social ministries. Ironically, Miss Farmer had been praying for God to send a missionary "couple" to Montgomery long before she received the invitation herself. But now the excitement of such an enormous challenge and the flood of peace from the Holy Spirit convinced her that this "couple" consisted of God and her. So she went.

Restoration for Dedication

Soon after moving to Montgomery, Miss Farmer wrote a letter to all the pastors in the association asking for volunteers to clean and repair the building for service. Even though the chapel remained in good condition, the entire building was overdue for a thorough cleaning and painting. Without the knowledge of the previous owners, derelicts had entered the building at night and desecrated it with truckloads of trash.

As Gladys scrubbed windows she prayed fervently that both those derelicts and the God-fearing Jews who built the synagogue might experience the personal and eternal cleansing made possible through Jesus the Messiah.

Very soon after the work opened, Miss Farmer gave a coffee to show about one hundred Baptist women the newly purchased building. Instead of the hostess cleaning up before the guests arrived, Miss Farmer invited the ladies to pick rooms they would like to return to clean up!

All of this work was new to many who had contributed money to missions all their lives. But here was a real live missionary asking them personally to get involved in home missions right in their own city.

Some of the ladies observed the new missionary from a distance at first, noticing how she keeps her hair in a modest French twist and usually wears shirtwaist dresses with a long shell necklace. Her hands look experienced, like those of a nurse, and her soft soprano voice automatically inspires others to dedication with clear enunciation and limitless life stories of people the Lord is patiently working upon.

With a serene and controlled spirit, sometimes she has to pause a moment during a conversation, as if she's breathing a prayer about the situation being discussed. With genteel politeness, she speaks the truth unashamedly and has a tenacity that would make Satan shudder when she's defending the rights of all people for compassion.

Fortunately God guides her to use those strengths to fight the forces of evil, which instills confidence in the downtrodden who come to trust her. "If I could have only one person to pray for me," one person said, "it would be Gladys Farmer."

Yet with genuine modesty she continually reflects all praise to God, who is both her strength and her joy.

Many of the people meeting Miss Farmer for the first time have to learn from experience that, rare as it is, total commitment *is* possible. Gladys Farmer lives it. Granted, not many people are so willing or able to give themselves totally to God's work in such self-sacrifice, but God blesses all who do in ways many people never experience.

If one word could describe these ladies' first impression of Gladys Farmer, it would be the same word they use after many more years of association with her: *committed* unto the Lord and all he wants her to do.

During the guided tour for these ladies, Miss Farmer described the future activities planned for each room. She talked about them just as if she could look in and see those activities taking place. Visualizing such scenes took much more imagination from these ladies who saw more problems than potential. But they went along with her dream and eventually started believing in the possibilities just as much as she did.

And it worked! Between seventy-five and one hundred volunteers returned with enthusiasm. Work groups representing many different churches bounded in with able backs, strong stomachs, and great energy, believing God needed even these talents in the teamwork of leading souls to Christ.

With well-worn brooms, floppy mops, many colors of paint, and battle-scarred paintbrushes, this happy bucket brigade restored a firetrap of a building into a caring center for broken souls.

For the first time many realized that they could give God their talents for manual labor, even when they couldn't teach a class. Men and boys loved this introduction into missions—works that needed their actions as well as their words.

Miss Farmer profusely praised the workers and repeatedly described this as a truly "caring" association. As a bonus, God gave these new volunteers a greater appreciation for total worldwide missions because they understood what missions is all about—people helping people because of Christ.

After three hectic months of cleaning, with joy the Montgomery Baptist Association dedicated the building and its work to the Lord on Sunday, May 21, 1972. Representatives of the Home Mission Board, the state Baptist Executive Board, and the Montgomery Baptist Association and over two hundred pastors and laymen came to declare their support and to pray that this work would bring honor and praise to the name of Jesus Christ. Just as Jesus shared the Scriptures in the synagogue and then walked out among the people with needs, Montgomery Baptists realized, "So must we."

4
Preparing the Ground

Ever since work began in the Baptist Center of Montgomery, the pace has fluctuated between "constant" and "crisis," depending upon the needs of the people.

The "constant" involves:
- Phone calls on a multitude of subjects
- Sundry requests at the door
- Meals on Wheels
- Tuesday Family Night
- Adult classes on Thursday morning
- Crafts and Bible study for children after school
- Guidance for volunteers
- Counseling and visits in homes
- Cooperation with other service agencies
- SON-shine Coffeehouse on Saturday night
- Many Vacation Bible Schools during the summer
- Speaking engagements in churches upon request.

The more numerous "crises" range anywhere from gathering clothes for the victims of a house fire to arranging an emergency trip to the hospital for someone. Baptist Center volunteers and missionaries always attempt to weave every action together with a witness to Christ with the hope of rescuing troubled lives not only from their most obvious difficulties but by meeting their deepest needs.

Passing the Word

Soon after the dedication of the building, volunteers knocked on doors around the inner city to accomplish their first priority: to discover the needs of the community. They told each person they visited what the Baptist Center hoped to do and invited everyone to attend the classes that were now forming. At each house they left a paper stating the times of each opportunity and the address and phone number of this new Christian social ministry.

After knocking on one door, volunteers heard a high, thin voice call for them to come in. At first they hesitated, but the voice was insistent.

Across the dimly lit room they saw a frail, white-haired woman lying on a very high bed. She seemed eager for company and with accented speech talked freely about her childhood in Lebanon and the death of her husband.

The volunteers offered her a leaflet and invited her to visit the Baptist Center. But she refused, explaining that she could not read and did not have a phone. They encouraged her to keep the paper anyway, saying, "If you ever need help you could ask a neighbor to call Miss Farmer at this number. She wants to be your friend." After consenting, she asked them to put the paper on the table beside the door as they left.

Several days later the elderly woman became very ill and repeatedly cried out for help. Her nearest neighbors were deaf, so no one came.

After suffering helplessly on the floor for many hours, she remembered the paper that the volunteers had encouraged her to keep. Using her arms, she dragged herself slowly and painfully across the room, finally reaching the table beside the door. Then, with all the strength she could muster, she waved the piece of paper in front of the window and continued to call out.

Finally a young man in a pickup truck slowed down in front of her house and heard her screams for help. After coming to investigate, he realized that the situation was more serious than he could handle. But he did agree to drive around to the Baptist Center and tell Miss Farmer how badly the woman needed help.

The missionary went immediately and stayed with the lady until she was comfortably back in bed. During her many days of recovery, Miss Farmer and Baptist Center volunteers strengthened the Lebanese lady with friendship and love rare to this woman shunned by many for running a house of prostitution years ago.

Because of her past sins, many failed to see the desperation of a widow starving for friendship who was unable to read or write and who lacked any skills for earning a respectable livelihood. No one had offered to help her learn to read or even to refer her to a place where she could.

Her little dog was her only companion, and even he experienced the opposite extremes of the lady's emotions. Like so many, this Lebanese lady's loneliness and needs went far deeper than just for contact with people and training in skills. No one had cared enough to tell her about God's love until Gladys Farmer shared the gospel with her. After receiving Christ at the age of eighty-two, the Lebanese lady *finally* felt loved.

Later this new believer became one of the many shut-ins who receive a lunch prepared by rotating Baptist churches on Tuesday. This meal began as a fellowship time for the inner-city elderly to come to the Baptist Center to eat, but the declining health of many caused the program to shift to a "Meals on Wheels" service, in which volunteers carry the lunches to their homes.

Many friendships have blossomed from this time of sharing; and volunteers often return to visit the elderly, even when it's not their day to deliver meals. The ones who do this learn that shared love multiplies into blessing for both the givers and the receivers.

Teaching for Prevention

Sometime later the Lebanese lady's house was scheduled to be torn down as part of an urban renewal project. Miss

Farmer offered to make some phone calls to help her find another place to live. But on her limited income, the only thing they could find within her range was an apartment in one of the federal housing projects.

As workers from Community Action and the Baptist Center helped her move, Miss Farmer observed with great concern the deplorable neighborhood conditions where the Lebanese lady would have to live. Broken bottles, rain-soaked litter, and empty cans cluttered the grass. Playground equipment was limited for the wandering children, who were using foul language. Overcrowding was quite obvious. In places slums were already being made of many fairly new modern brick apartments.

After they had finished settling the Lebanese lady in her new surroundings, Miss Farmer returned impatiently to the Baptist Center to call the Montgomery Housing Authority, requesting permission to hold neighborhood Bible classes under the tree in the new resident's yard.

The man who answered the call suggested that they continue their conversation in a conference hookup with J. C. Miller, executive director of the Montgomery Housing Authority. Mr. Miller said that the combination of crafts and Bible study sounded like an answered prayer to him because he and many others in their office had become concerned and frustrated by the complexity of the problems in the projects. They had prayed for God's help to meet the residents' needs in these communities.

Overwhelming hardly describes the needs among the people in Montgomery's twenty federal housing projects. Because the rent is based upon income, between 20 and 25 percent pay less than ten dollars a month. But abuse of the buildings often causes them to pay enormous utility bills.

Illiteracy, unemployment, alcoholism, adultery, and other problems breed quickly in this atmosphere of frustration and despair. The welfare workers have tried to help,

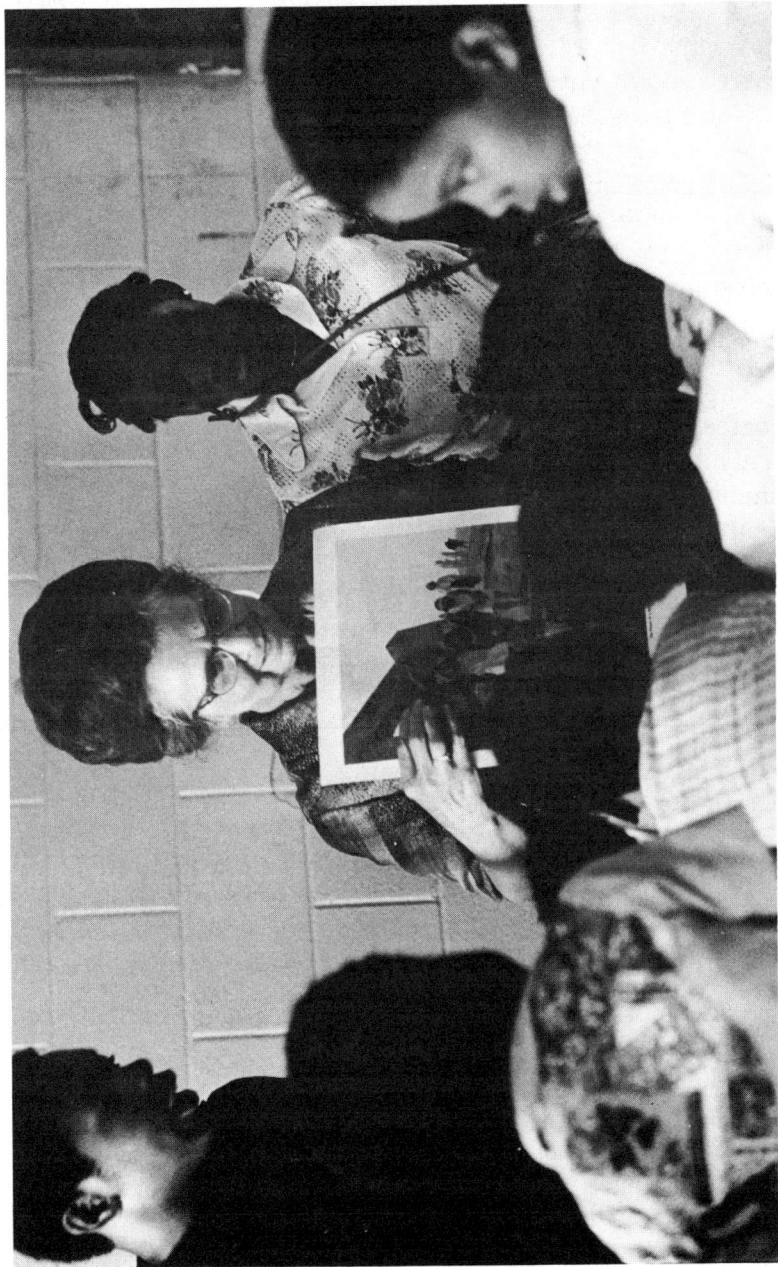

Total attendance in all Baptist Center-sponsored programs climaxed at 10,855 just for June and July of 1979. (Photo by Don Rutledge, Home Mission Board, SBC)

but some factors actually encourage people to remain in their present circumstances.

Volunteers have learned that much immorality stems from inability to read the Bible. More than once they have heard comments such as, "I'm gonna have another baby to get more money." Yet the mother gives very little thought to the constant needs which that child will have for years to come. When the people are lovingly shown some of the Scriptures pertaining to adultery, many say they've never heard what God said about that.

The responsibility of teaching for both prevention and correction must be shared by the concerned church which truly believes that a relationship with Jesus Christ can change lives, both now and forever. And the formative years of childhood proves to be the most opportune time to start.

The first Baptist Center-sponsored Bible study in the Montgomery housing projects began under a tree in the Lebanese lady's new yard. As student missionary James Anderson strummed his guitar, over eighty children gathered around and heard him tell about the prodigal son.

Since that time, other housing areas have invited the Baptist Center to use their community centers and yards for this program which combines crafts, songs, and stories from God's Word. Almost everyone who has taught in situations such as these comes away amazed by these children, who thirst for love and beg the teachers to stay longer when it's time to go. How rewarding it is to see children sharing more and practicing kindness among themselves.

One day after classes had ended, a maintenance man was busy repairing a broken window when a young fellow walked up and started talking. "You ever heard of a man named Jesus?" he asked. The maintenance man nodded, so the youngster started talking to him. "I jus' thought 'Jesus' was a bad word, not a real person. That teacher even said he died for me."

We must never assume that everyone has heard the gospel. Teaching the Bible in neighborhoods such as these is one of the best ways to make sure they do.

Reaching Out

Many of the afternoon Bible studies started with Vacation Bible School in the summer. In many ways these mission Vacation Bible Schools are like those conducted in churches, yet with a lot more flexibility. But anyone who has ever worked in just one Vacation Bible School can only slightly imagine the preparation it takes to conduct more than thirty-three mission Bible Schools within ten weeks!

Early preparation for each involves the following:

1. Observe areas of need scarcely touched by community churches, housing projects, mobile home parks, or apartment complexes. Then contact the key person to ask permission for conducting a VBS there, explaining who you are and what a mission VBS would involve. Many owners or supervisors of an area appreciate planned activities for the children. And the character stories and Bible training might produce better tenants and less vandalism.

2. Secure volunteers and plan with them. The "Big A Club," published by Woman's Missionary Union, and the Backyard Bible Study materials, as well as the regular VBS materials published by the Sunday School Board of the Southern Baptist Convention, can all be used in mission situations. Good planning is vital for a smoothly run school.

3. Prepare leaflets, containing the date, time, and type of activities, for distribution in the area on Thursday or Friday before VBS begins on Monday. Volunteers can often get energetic children to pass the leaflets out while they encourage mothers to allow their children to attend.

4. Arrive early on the first day so that playing children will see you and join the crowd. Often a strolling guitarist or children holding the two flags signals the starting time to others. Sometimes it's also necessary to go early enough

to pick up broken bottles, etc., that could hurt barefooted children.

The joint worship is often modified from what might be practiced in churches because of the lack of a piano and the students' limited knowledge of songs. Leaders can hold up large posters containing words to simple choruses and use flipchart pictures to accompany the character stories.

After a time of joint worship, they break up into smaller groups sitting on woven bedspreads for more personal attention with crafts and deeper Bible study. If they don't have a Bible they can bring from home, the Baptist Center gives them one made possible by Christmas in August gifts or through the Gideons.

All teaching includes a discussion of the ways we can apply the Scriptures to daily living. Most of the children eagerly participate and go away with real spiritual food in addition to the punch and cookies.

As public school reopens in the fall, the Baptist Center tries to continue its ministry in as many areas as they have enough volunteers who are willing to teach. But since many more homemakers have taken full-time employment in the past five years and many teenage student teachers can only help in the summer, there are more areas needing Bible studies than there are Christians willing or able to go.

One afternoon as Miss Farmer went to one of the housing project community centers to teach for an absent volunteer, she found a twelve-year-old early arriver shoving chairs across the highly polished floor just to see the teachers and pupils jump as they entered the room.

She quickly but calmly asked him to come outside. A few minutes later, stomping the ground and a little angry, he asked, "We gonna have anything good for Easter?"

"Yes, we always do," she answered. "We'll study about Jesus dying on the cross."

"I know that cross," he said as if to cut her off.

"But the cross is not all," she continued. "Jesus also came out of the grave."

"Who come out of the grave?" he huffed, somewhat troubled.

So she shared the meaning of Jesus' death and resurrection, beginning with the child's experiences. "Robert, have you ever known anybody who died?"

After he told her how both his granddaddy and little cousin had died, the missionary explained that the spirits of his cousin and grandfather were now with the Lord if they were Christians. She explained further that one day their bodies will also come forth and be changed to new bodies by Jesus himself and that the Christians still living will go to be with the Lord in heaven too.

The lad responded with total seriousness. "If that's really true, I wanna be a Christian too!" That day he accepted Christ as his Savior and continues to be a witness in his neighborhood.

He throws no more chairs because now he's too busy bringing his friends to sit in them so that they can hear the same truths that have changed his life.

The SON-shine Coffeehouse on Saturday night was organized as another opportunity primarily for inner-city youth to hear about Jesus in a relaxed atmosphere of guitar music, extemporaneous testimonies, and fellowship around large tables. But when one youth asked Miss Farmer if he could bring his mother, she certainly couldn't refuse.

After years of ignoring God, his mother surprised even herself by agreeing to come. Long ago, even though she was not a Christian herself, she had prayed for God to spare the life of her alcoholic father. When her father died anyway, she turned against God and refused to pray again. Until then she had firmly kept that promise.

But during her early experience in the Baptist Center Coffeehouse, the Holy Spirit penetrated the hardness of her heart, then her son's; and together they hurried to the prayer room, asking for God's forgiveness and saving grace.

On Thursday morning other ladies participate in programs that combine Bible study with sewing, nutrition, crochet, or other activities in several different locations. During the same time their preschoolers enjoy learning activities geared to their own special needs.

Many of these children come from such deprived environments that they have to be taught how to hold a pencil or use a crayon. Many consider fruit a special treat and before now seldom gave thanks before eating. With wide eyes filled with wonder they explore puzzles and enjoy the pictures that teachers show during Bible study time.

In order to minister to the rapidly changing western side of town, the Montgomery Baptist Association opened a Christian kindergarten, Mother's Club, and activities for boys at Westgate Baptist Church. After most of their members moved to other communities, the remaining congregation decided to disband and deed their building, land, and pastorium to the Montgomery Baptist Association for continued use of those facilities for mission work in that area.

The work grew under excellent leadership and eventually evolved into what is now known as Westside Baptist Mission, sponsored by Trinity Baptist Church. Rev. Milton Boyd, who was a member of Trinity Baptist and had already volunteered his services through the Family Nights at the Baptist Center, came as pastor to Westside. With the help of thirteen other Trinity members he reorganized the existing programs into the mission organizations of Southern Baptist churches.

During the Thursday night activities, Westside also offers literacy training. A volunteer trained in the Laubach method now teaches reading to an eighty-year-old black woman, who says she "always wanted to learn to read." Her young granddaughter started coming just to sit, but absorbed so much from listening that she could read before starting to school.

At a recent gathering of volunteers the grandmother read aloud from Sunday School leaflets with graded vocabulary and gave her testimony of the joy she felt to even be able to write down an emergency telephone message for a neighbor. Just imagine all that one misses without the ability to read and write! How appreciative she was to the dedicated Christian lady who took time to teach her how!

Some 1,033 professions of faith resulted from the witness of the Baptist Center between 1972 and 1979. Most of these were people seldom exposed to the gospel at any other time—people whom many ignore because they are thought to be too difficult to reach.

Whether sharing the gospel happens during a Vacation Bible School in the summer, during neighborhood Bible studies after school, in one of the discussions during Family Night, through counseling, or because of any other opportunity, God promises, "So shall my word be that goeth forth out of my mouth: it shall not return unto me void, but it shall accomplish that which I please, and it shall prosper in the thing whereto I sent it" (Isa. 55:11).

Responding to Requests

The crisis requests have included such things as carrying jugs of water to a shut-in whose pipes burst in cold weather and providing a cot and groceries for a lady whose brother was coming to her house that day after spending thirty-five years in prison.

While helping with the needs of the parolee's sister, Miss Farmer learned that her brother had been led to the Lord by a Christian who witnessed to him in prison. The missionary used this opportunity to ask the woman if she too had accepted Christ as her Savior.

"No, I ain't," she said quite frankly, but with an expression that reflected an eagerness to learn. So Miss Farmer gently showed the woman Scriptures that told her how she could also receive Christ into her heart, which she did through prayer. Even though evangelism is one of the main goals of missions, the work also includes serving others in time of need.

Whenever an unfortunate experience happens away from home, Christians can depend upon a Baptist Center for help. One of many examples includes a family who was en route to a new home in another state when their car caught on fire while they were passing through Montgomery. The money they had for gas was soon used up in towing their car off the interstate to a garage, one night of unexpected motel expenses, and two days of food while the local garage tried to restore their defective car. Two other nights of lodging had also been supplied by the Salvation Army.

After they arrived on the doorsteps of the Baptist Center, the missionary staff combined efforts to work out their problem, transported them to get their car out of the shop, and invited them to share lunch with the friends who gathered to celebrate Miss Farmer's sixty-fifth birthday party at noon, February 14, 1979.

Because of the interstate chain, Montgomery is a thoroughfare for people going in many different directions. Migrants come through while heading south to pick crops. And many Northerners come south during the winter to escape the ice and snow. The presence of many historical attractions and the fact that Montgomery is the hub of state government cause many to visit and seek work here. Many hungry transients knock on the Baptist Center's door daily.

The Center's staff and volunteers who hear their requests do intake records on each one that include the name, address, number of family members, place of employment or other source of income, specific request, church affiliation, etc. During this time of getting to know the person the volunteer can witness as they talk and encourage him to attend Bible study at the Baptist Center or a church near his home.

One day as Miss Farmer talked to a transient who

smelled of alcohol but had asked for food, his companion, who had not been drinking, was standing outside her office door and straining to hear the verses of Scripture that she shared.

Just after she said, "Him that cometh to me, I will in no wise cast out" (John 6:37), the friend came in and said with total sincerity, "Hey, say it again. I think that one's for me."

So the missionary asked the uninterested man to sit outside her office door, and she continued sharing other Scriptures with the one grasping for God's will in his life. And God did come in. Just as he promised, his Word will not return void.

Ministering in the Home

One of the most frustrating aspects of Baptist Center work is that so many people knock at the door that Miss Farmer can't visit in homes as much as she would like. But she does the best she can (between two hundred and five hundred visits a year). Most of these come during her "time off," weekends and holidays. But she feels that by visiting in the homes she can minister in a more personal way than is usually possible during a class or amid the interruptions of her daily routine.

On one occasion she made a special effort to visit an older couple who had been receiving Baptist Center lunches on Tuesday. The woman had made a profession of faith during a Family Night, but the man had never come.

During the missionary's visit in the home they openly admitted that they were living together without being married. God gave Miss Farmer a tactful boldness to show them the Scriptures teaching God's disapproval of adultery. The woman repented and asked for God's forgiveness.

But the man refused to marry her, saying that they could not survive without the two federal checks that their present arrangement allowed; besides, he felt he would be sinning more to marry someone with her "past."

She separated herself from him for a while, but relatives and friends still avoided her. Sick and lonely, the woman eventually returned to the man, who still refused marriage. But the conviction of the Holy Spirit made her constantly miserable. The snare of sin hurts until people actually beg to get out of their problems.

Finally the crippled woman persuaded the common-law husband to take her to the Baptist Center, giving him some excuse which he agreed to. Once they were inside she "floored" him with the statement, "I want to make a clean break with sin. I'm not going to live with anybody I'm not married to."

With Miss Farmer standing there overhearing the conversation, there wasn't much he could do but walk out. Miss Farmer helped the lady to be placed in a nearby nursing home. Now after years of sin and guilt she wanted to start fulfilling her promise to Jesus that she would "go and sin no more."

While some situations can be improved, at other times people just need the strength to cope with the present. By visiting in one terminally ill patient's home, Miss Farmer learned that two factors plagued this cancer patient's mind. In addition to the fear of dying, she felt a frantic urgency to get help for a nearly deaf grandson who shared her home.

Through assistance from other service agencies Miss Farmer got medical help for the boy and saw his grades improve as a result. After she made repeated visits to read Scriptures that strengthened the dying woman, on one trip the lady smiled and said, "I'm not afraid anymore. I'm ready to go whenever the Lord wants to take me." Strength to cope with the present is one of the greatest gifts that a Christian can share. But the best gift is eternity.

5
Tools and Laborers

"Talented? Who, me?"

This reply often comes from some of the most gifted people, who mistakenly reserve the word *talent* only for those with special skills or unusual aptitudes. But today talent includes much more than skill.

The Greek word translated *talent* means weight or balance. A talent during Jesus' earthly days meant a weight of money, as described in Matthew 25:14-30. This well-known parable tells how the master not only blessed those who multiplied their talents but also provided them with additional responsibilities because they had been faithful with little.

Today the word talent has been expanded to include more than money or the goods that money can buy. It also means time, skills, and personality. Whatever we have and whatever we do we can give to God, who will multiply it.

The ministry of a Baptist Center can use practically any talent of time, resource, or personality that anyone of any age wants to give for the glory of God. Even people who don't feel especially skilled can offer their time to sit with shut-ins who need someone to listen to them talk. Christians who consider themselves unqualified to teach might share a can of food regularly or baby-sit for others who want to teach. Those with the ability to teach are always in demand.

Small Staff

With an enrollment of over 3,000 in twenty-seven different areas in the summer and at least twenty areas in the winter, it is difficult to comprehend all the needs that such a work includes. It would be impossible for a paid staff to do all the work alone. But at the same time, volunteers must have someone to guide them to the needs that exist and coordinate so large a work.

During the first six years after the Montgomery Baptist Center was begun, the paid staff consisted only of Missionary Gladys Farmer and temporary assistance in several different forms.

Two US-2 missionary couples have served at different intervals: first Mayson and Mary Easterling and then Phillip and Sheila Duncan. The term US-2er applies to people appointed by the Home Mission Board to serve within the United States for two years.

The opportunities of service at a Baptist Center vary according to the requests of the moment, so student assistants soon learn that their duties remain flexible. They just practice Ecclesiastes 9:10: "Whatsoever thy hand findeth to do, do it with thy might."

Leaders in a Baptist Center always try to make the best possible use of volunteers' contributions of time, resources, and abilities. They try to link Christians with special gifts to people with special needs.

Whenever necessary, Gladys Farmer goes with a volunteer for the first time or until he can serve alone. The harder volunteers work, the harder she works. No job is too dirty or demanding for this dedicated leader who would never ask a volunteer to do something she wouldn't do herself—and usually has done on countless other occasions.

God gave Miss Farmer the wisdom to trust volunteers with responsibility, and she prays constantly for God to teach them along the way. Even though sometimes it would be easier to do a job herself, she tries to exercise patience so they can experience the joy of service.

But Satan tempts volunteers, and all Christians, with the same ferocity with which he tries to defeat missionaries. Anyone wishing to farm the inner city for Christ must maintain a strong spirit of commitment and stay focused on God's leadership and consider every effort a service to the Lord.

Missionary of the Day

Miss Farmer served as a missionary thirty-one years before enjoying the assistance of a regular paid staff secretary. In January of 1978 the Montgomery Baptist Association hired Mrs. Mary Mangham to work twenty hours a week. But already, as do many others who love this work, she gives much more than is expected.

In all the years before hiring a secretary, the Baptist Center used volunteers who usually came only one morning a week to answer the phone or doorbell, work in the clothing room, type whenever possible, and serve as the general flunkies that Baptist Center staffers appreciatively call Missionaries of the Day.

Many volunteers originally responded after hearing about the needs in one of Miss Farmer's seventy-five to one hundred speaking engagements throughout the year in various churches. Mrs. Evie Shoemaker volunteered to become her first Montgomery Missionary of the Day after hearing the new missionary speak in a worship service at Coosada.

Like many other people, Mrs. Shoemaker said that long before the Baptist Center came she felt very uncomfortable hearing about missions and doing so little. She wanted to get personally involved. So the call for volunteers at the newly opened Baptist Center sounded like answered prayer to this one so eager to help others.

After Mrs. Shoemaker enthusiastically shared each day's

experiences with her husband, he often commented on his own desire to help. But his job demanded long hours that prevented him from teaching in the housing project as she did or in the Baptist Center itself. So he supported his wife with the encouragement that all servants of God need from their individual families.

But Mr. Shoemaker continued to look for other ways to help missions and found one. With his Christmas bonus he and his wife bought a washer and dryer and gave it to the Baptist Center.

And how they've been used! No washateria operates within walking distance of the Baptist Center, so many people, too poor to afford a washer in their home, have a struggle to stay clean.

The bedspreads used for small-group time on the grass during mission Vacation Bible Schools must be washed daily so they will be ready to go again in the morning.

Many sick shut-ins have also benefited from this special service given by the people who picked up their dirty laundry and returned it to them clean.

God gives everyone talents—to some a few, to others very many. Then he waits to see how we will let him multiply them in the soil of the world.

Food and Clothes

Other volunteers see the need for sorting and sizing the clothes that people generously give to the Baptist Center. Perhaps a few words of advice might help at both ends:

1. Many people ask what is needed. Children's clothes are always in demand. But needy adults often request sizes different than what most have contributed. This inner-city ministry tends to involve more stout women and slim men than many people realize.

2. The efficiency and accuracy of volunteers in the clothing room can be greatly improved if contributors will pin the size in the neck or waistband of garments that lack

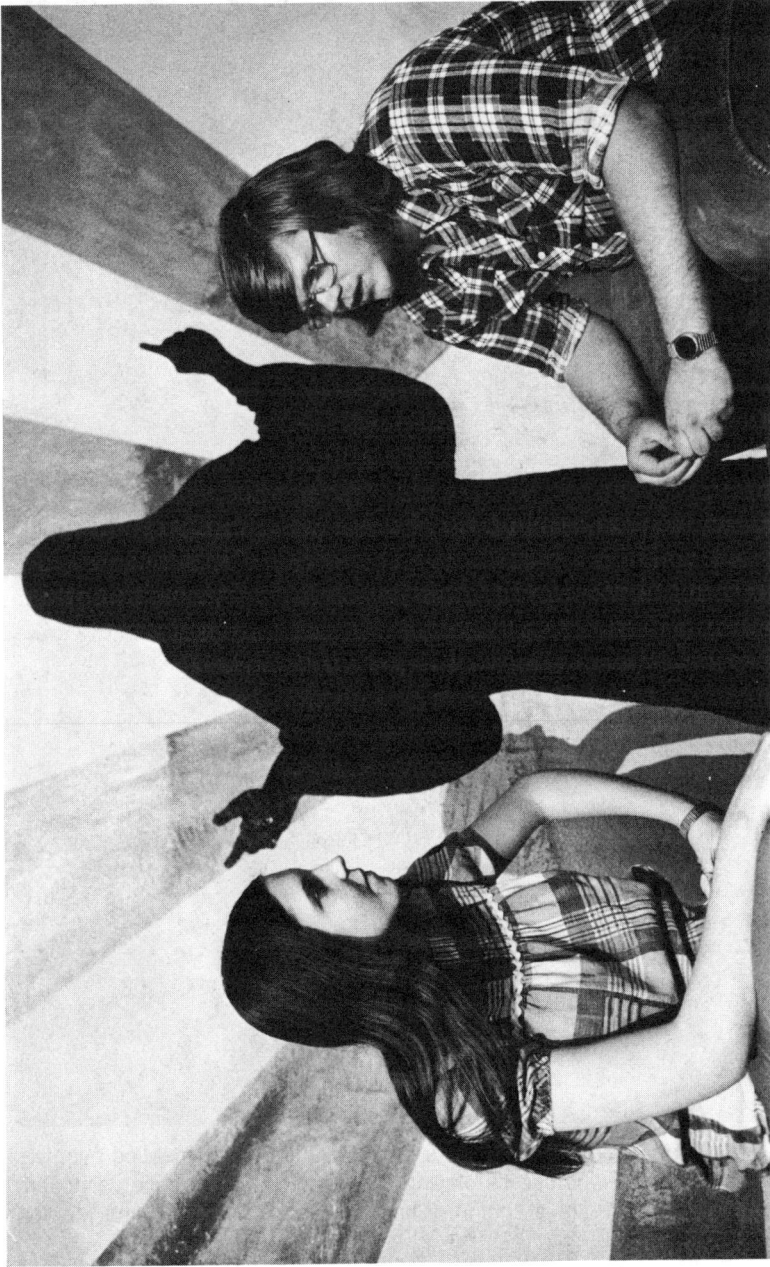

Teenage rap session in the coffeehouse focuses on the importance of Jesus as center of our lives. (Photo by Don Rutledge, Home Mission Board, SBC)

Gladys Farmer teaches volunteers to share Christ while meeting people's physical needs—whether it's playing basketball with a juvenile delinquent or cutting toenails for a shut-in. (Photo by Don Rutledge, Home Mission Board, SBC)

size labels. Unfortunately, sometimes people send clothes that need extensive repairs to give to people who cannot afford a sewing machine and often lack the skills for sewing by hand. Several volunteers have helped make minor repairs in order for a garment to be used, but this delays meeting a need.

3. Clothes given to a Baptist Center become tools for the ministry. So Christians should always consider whether they would be proud to wear this garment themselves or whether they could cheerfully witness while presenting it to someone else.

Housecoats and bed linens also find homes easily, especially among shut-ins. Unexpected hospitalizations cause many to request gowns, pajamas, and slippers in good condition.

Victims of house fires often come to the Baptist Center for clothes, and many appreciate the spiritual encouragement they receive at the same time. One such example involved the family of a young fireman whose own rented home suffered a nighttime electrical fire while he was at work—just a few days before Christmas.

Fortunately, his wife got herself and their three young children to safety in the nick of time. Dressed only in their sleepwear, this young mother and her children watched everything, even their Christmas gifts, dissolve into ashes.

The next morning a Christian neighbor brought her to the Baptist Center to get clothes for the entire family. Miss Farmer was happy to share what Baptist people had brought for such a time of need.

As they gathered clothes, the missionary asked the young woman if she had ever received the Christ who could strengthen her through not only that experience but for the rest of her life as well. The young mother replied that this was something she had put off much too long, but she really wanted to know how she could.

Miss Farmer shared some appropriate Scriptures with

her, and the lady prayed for Christ to come into her life as both Lord and Savior. Several days later the young mother told a friend: "As I watched everything we worked so hard for just go up in smoke, I doubted whether any good could ever come from something so terrible. But now I can actually thank God that it happened. Without experiencing a time of need, I might have forever ignored the one thing I needed most."

Volunteers often comment on the way that work through the Baptist Center opens their eyes to appreciate things they always took for granted. Two ladies who volunteered to take some supplies to a man recently released from the hospital relate the following experience.

The elderly man was obviously very sick and very appreciative that they had taken the time to come. When they told him they were delivering a sack of things that the Baptist Center thought he might could use, he asked if maybe the contents included a pair of shoes.

They had not yet examined the contents of the sack; but when they opened it and took out a pair of shoes, he broke out in sobs and thanked them profusely.

These volunteers experienced great joy in sharing that needed pair of shoes and wished that whoever supplied them could have also seen the expression of gratitude beaming from his face.

But God used the goodwill of both the supplier and those who delivered it to bless someone with both physical and spiritual needs.

Food is probably the most frequently requested item at the Baptist Center. Even in this day of both food stamps and welfare checks, inflation decreases the quantity of food that people can buy on fixed incomes.

Miss Farmer laughingly comments, "Jesus multiplied food for the people, but the Baptist Center has to divide." When the Baptist Center first opened, two Christian businessmen jointly gave one thousand dollars as an emergency

A sweet spirit of cooperation grows as volunteers serve together. (Photo by Don Rutledge, Home Mission Board, SBC)

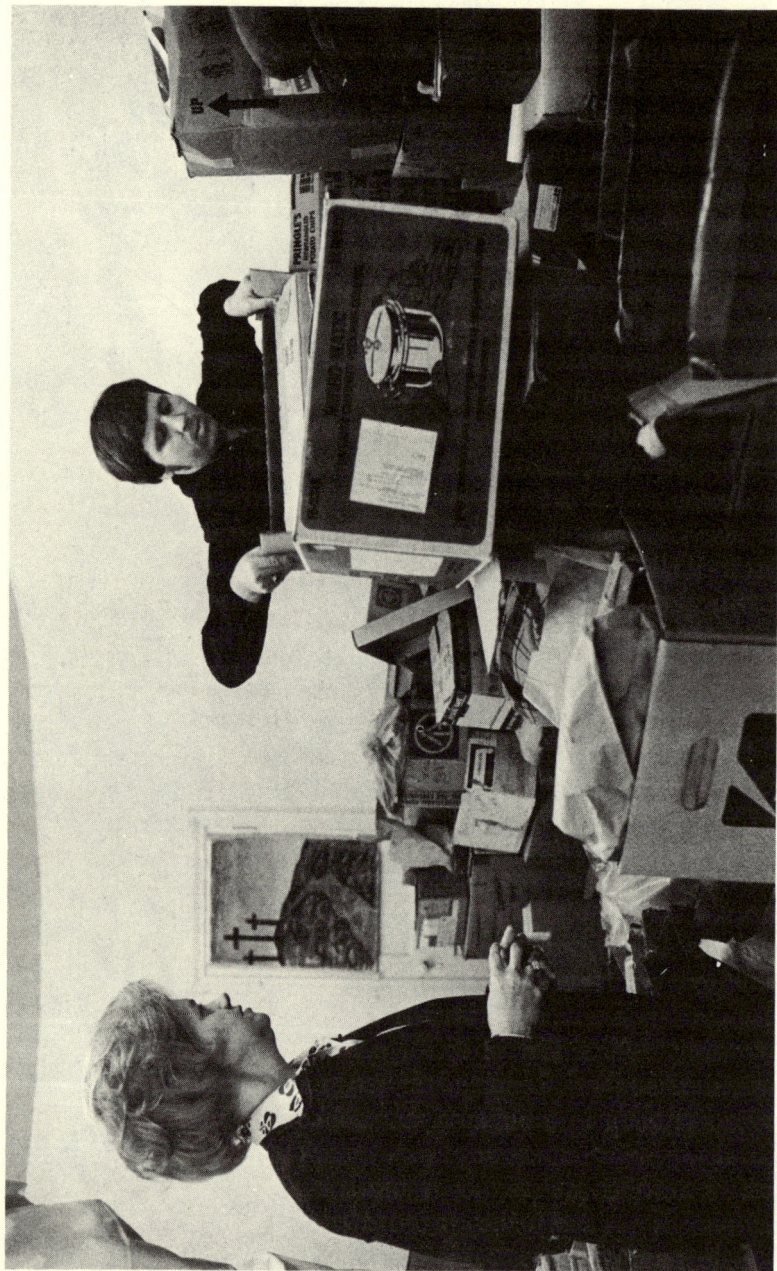

Volunteers sort many necessary things in order to free the missionary to counsel people. (Photo by Don Rutledge, Home Mission Board, SBC)

fund to cover food requests after the cupboard became bare. This amount was stretched over five years prior to exhaustion—thanks to other food brought by various mission groups and individual Christians.

Staples that are always needed to keep the pantry stocked include the following:

> Powdered milk (3 qt. or 8 qt. size)
> Canned meats (tuna, stew, etc.)
> Canned soups, vegetables, and fruit
> Self-rising flour and meal
> Syrup and jelly
> Cereal (12 or 16 oz.)
> Cheese spread in a jar
> Oatmeal
> Sugar
> Rice (1 lb.)
> Dried beans
> Grits
> Shortening
> Spaghetti (1 lb.)
> Peanut butter
> Crackers

Each person who receives a sack of food from the Baptist Center is also encouraged to return for the Bible studies. Some do; some don't. But those who come asking for food also receive a witness they wouldn't get in most secular agencies.

One instance in which a need for food provided a ministry involved a woman whom a volunteer found crying on the Baptist Center steps even before it opened. In talking to her, the Christian heard how the woman's husband had recently left her for a younger woman. This left her alone to raise a young granddaughter whose mother had been killed.

The grandmother's poor eyesight prevented her from getting a job in the only skill she knew, sewing. She had no money to buy glasses, and the long red tape of being processed for federal assistance programs would take several more days. On the morning she came to the Baptist Center, she had already mopped a neighbor's floors to get her granddaughter a breakfast at their table.

Through the Baptist Center this lady got a referral and glasses through the Lion's Club, plus food for the two of them from the Baptist Center until their check started. She admitted she had not attended church in a very long time but said she would now go back.

Since that time she has acquired a regular job and now supports herself. But the Baptist Center was there in her time of need.

Men in Missions

In most communities, women lead out in missions. But a Baptist Center also involves many men who give of their talents in the cause of Christ.

From the earliest days of the Baptist Center in Montgomery, men have helped to put, and keep, the building in shape for classes that are conducted there. Much painting, plastering, rewiring, and building shelves have made the former synagogue both serviceable and inviting to people who seldom considered church attendance before.

Several have trimmed the shrubbery to allow more light to come through the windows. Other men erected the sign that shares the gospel in itself. "Believe on the Lord Jesus Christ, and thou shalt be saved" is read by countless passersby throughout the day.

Soon after the sign was erected, a passing young Jewish man came in and said, "I see my star of David over the door and a cross out by the sign in the yard! Pray tell, what goes on here—a Baptist work in a Jewish synagogue?" Missionary Gladys Farmer was delighted by the opportunity to share the purpose of this ministry with one who also loved righteousness and invited him to receive Jesus the Messiah as his atoning Savior.

Many men have squeezed precious time out of very busy schedules in order to help others through different ministries of the Baptist Center. One man takes part of his lunch hour once a week to share a devotional with the elderly who gather for a government lunch program in a local Catholic church (government food in a Catholic church blessed with a Baptist witness). And the people beg for him to stay longer!

The two vans used for transportation could not have survived without the attention of men who used their mechanical talents for the glory of God. Others offer their services by driving multiple routes to pick up people who come to the classes. After one realizes how few of the participants in Baptist Center programs own cars, or could get to these excellent classes any other way, these talents for driving become essential tools for sharing the gospel with people.

A few men make themselves available for running whatever errands might arise. This ranges anywhere from picking up food stamps for persons unable to do so for themselves to moving someone into a different apartment.

The two vans were supplied with offerings that Christians made to the Montgomery Baptist Association. (Many churches give a percentage of their total budget to the association as a cooperative ministry.)

The vans have provided services that have helped many people from the very first day of their arrival. On the evening after the first one came, Miss Farmer took an opportunity to accustom herself to the clutch before time to leave for a speaking engagement in her own car.

It was already dark when the headlights revealed a lady sprawled on the sidewalk, so she stopped to see if she could help. After getting closer, she recognized one of the elderly people to whom they took lunches on Tuesday.

The woman tried to get up, but her hip was obviously broken. Miss Farmer called an ambulance and stayed with her for three hours until the emergency room could locate her doctor. Needless to say, Miss Farmer had to cancel her speaking engagement at the last minute; but she prayed that the Christians would understand that on this occasion God wanted her actions rather than words.

Numerous businessmen have shared both their time and resources in many useful ways. This has included supplying and laying tile; doing heating, air-conditioning, and vent work; using their trucks for moving people, storage boxes, desks; expert advice; money for needy people; help with employment for some; and many other important and varied tasks that God knows and will reward.

Everything given to the Baptist Center is used to the best possible advantage. In fact, very seldom is anything thrown away. Much to the consternation of many meticulous homemakers who volunteer their services in the clothing room and elsewhere, Miss Farmer saves everything, expecting to use it in response to some need.

Once as US-2er Mary Easterling tied all matching shoes together, she came up with a whole box of shoes that had lost their mates. She thought surely she had now found something Miss Farmer would be willing to throw away.

But Miss Farmer just replied, "We must think of the one-legged people too."

And even though we don't encourage the contribution of any more single shoes, amazingly enough, some amputees around the city have benefited from this situation.

She gives such detailed accounting of Baptist Center expenditure to the association that one pastor commented that the nation would soon get out of the red if the president would name Gladys Farmer as National Budget Director. She believes that every cent belongs to God; and as his manager for this work, she stretches every penny to reach the greatest number of needs.

Busily Retired

A wealth of talents come from volunteers who are retired from jobs they once held but are willing to give their energy and experiences so others can come to Christ.

Miss Audrey Brown, an eighty-year-old volunteer, works as hard as a paid staff member in sharing her many different talents. She takes shorthand and types correspondence that Miss Farmer dictates in the morning and saves the missionary's time by answering the phone. On Thursday nights she teaches literacy classes at Westside mission as well as conversational English to internationals.

She has a lot of love to give and doesn't mind inconveniencing herself to do so. After Miss Brown invited one of her friends to also help through the Baptist Center, the friend shrugged off the suggestion with a comment about "at times she doesn't feel too well."

To this the redhead, with a long history of arthritis, just said, "Well, who doesn't have something wrong with them? We just have to face it and keep going."

A lot can be said for the stamina and strength of character that many retired persons possess. And as we face challenges today we can often benefit greatly from the wisdom that comes with experience. People in need feel comfortable around someone who they know has also experienced trials and sets a good example of how the Lord can pull us through those difficult times, making us even stronger than we were before.

Statistics often remind us that the older a person is before accepting Christ, the less likely he will ever do so. One exception involved a ninety-three-year-old man to whom some of these busily retired volunteers witnessed. He lived in a seven-story apartment complex for low-income senior citizens.

He refused to come to the Bible study in his building, but his brother accepted Christ when volunteers visited

him in a housing project. The ninety-three-year-old said,
"What happened to my brother? He's different, not as or-
nery as he used to be."

So they explained that his brother had asked Jesus to
come into his life and that Jesus makes the difference. As
time went on, two nurses and a teacher and her husband
ministered to his physical needs following a severe heart
attack and continued to witness to him. He then believed
and asked that a little cassette bearing his testimony be
mailed to his kinsfolk. This they did.

He asked to be carried in his wheelchair to the Bible
class to share this testimony: "I want you to know that I
am not the same man you have been seeing roll around
here. I turned to Jesus and he saved me. I do not know
why I waited until I was ninety-three, except that I was
hung up on being 'born again.' But I am not the only old
boy who had such a hang-up. That old boy Nicodemus did
too."

Then, seriously, he concluded: "From here on, until Jesus
calls me home, I am going to tell everybody I can about
Jesus."

Children and Youth

Unfortunately, childhood is often mistaken as a time of
waiting to "become something," even waiting until one is
"old enough" to serve the Lord as the adults do. This fallacy
never applies to work through a Baptist Center.

The quantity of letters that Miss Farmer receives proves
that this ministry is daily strengthened by the talents of
children praying for missions. The power of their prayers
should never be underestimated or overlooked. With all
these little prayer warriors, you might say Montgomery's
Baptist Center has volunteers in many different states.

Another way children contribute is through Christmas
in August gifts that provide material used in this work
all year long and presents for over 2,500 people enrolled

in various Bible classes. The gifts sent include such items as crayons, pencils, glue, games, toothbrushes, soap, combs and brushes, washcloths, Bibles, socks, scarves, and sewing material.

For Christmas 1978 the Baptist Center gave socks and notebook paper to at least two thousand children. This might not seem like such an exciting gift to children who only want toys and candy, but it was special to many children whose parents can't afford to buy as much paper or as many socks as they need for school.

With the help of many local churches, adults get a warm scarf or cap. About one hundred shut-ins also get gifts suited to their special needs.

In addition to gift-giving, the mission offers a wide range of possible actions for children. Children old enough to cut grass sometimes offer their talents to a shut-in too sick to care for his own yard. Others can read to blind persons or write a letter for them as they talk. Even drawing a picture or sending someone a card can cheer him up.

The first time children visit a shut-in they might feel unsure of what to say or do, but one sweet lady surprised a Vacation Bible School group by singing them a funny song that she once sang to children she baby-sat.

Some of the same children returned to this sweet lady's home again at Christmas to surprise her with Christmas carols outside her window. Their leader had heard that both she and her husband had the flu, so they didn't go in.

But the lady heard them and wept and blew kisses down to the singing children. They didn't understand the tears, but their tender hearts were touched and they sang even louder.

The next day Miss Farmer called the children's leader to ask if she would play for the husband's funeral—for the family where they had sung the day before. The missionary explained that, unknown to the carolers, the man had died several hours before they came.

Deep in grief, his widow wondered if she could possibly live alone without the husband she had loved so much. She prayed for God to send her a special sign if he wanted her to continue to live.

"Just after I prayed that prayer," she told Miss Farmer later in the funeral home, "an unexpected choir of angel children sang Christmas carols outside my window. I knew then that God would continue to give me the strength to keep on living and supply all my needs in the future."

Teenagers who help through the Baptist Center use their talents in many different ways. Soon after the building opened, a group from Eastern Hills Baptist Church came to prepare the basement for use as a coffeehouse. With energy and enthusiasm they scrubbed and painted while joking with each other.

Then one youth said, "What's the coffeehouse going to be named?"

Miss Farmer replied that the one in Phenix City was called Noah's Ark, but she was open to any suggestion they could offer. So many good ideas came out that they had to vote which one they liked best, and "SON-shine" Coffeehouse won overwhelmingly.

Then someone said the room decorations ought to reflect the name. Everyone immediately agreed and turned to the fellow so gifted in art. They liked what he suggested: a mural at the front of the room silhouetting the Son of God standing in front of rays of sunshine. This talent for art became a tool for God to share how light can enter a life when the Son of God shines in.

The majority of workers in the thirty-seven mission Vacation Bible Schools are also teenagers. They do an excellent job of sharing Jesus with children who have little exposure to the gospel message.

One girl commented, "Working in the housing projects has brought me closer to God in my own spiritual life. I guess I didn't fully appreciate what Jesus did for me until I started telling others what he wants to do for them."

Recreation and fellowship are important to Christian youth, but many grow tired of listening without putting those truths into action. Involvement in missions meets needs of those who give and those who receive. In addition to spreading the gospel, it gives youth something to do that's meaningful and rewarding. It reinforces what they've already learned when they practice each precept and share truths aloud with others.

Teaching others often uncovers gaps in their knowledge and sends them searching the Scriptures for answers to their questions. God saves people for service as well as for eternal security. And sometimes the service rendered by children and youth can reach those who might listen to their testimony when they wouldn't listen to adults.

Youth who are active for the Lord today usually grow into the Christian leaders of tomorrow. For that reason we should encourage their participation in missions as much as possible and express appreciation for what they've already done.

Gladys Farmer appreciates every effort by all ages and depends greatly upon their continued support, trusting that everyone has talents that can be used in missions.

Ephesians 4:11-12 reads, "And he gave some, apostles; and some, prophets; and some, evangelists; and some, pastors and teachers; For the perfecting of the saints, for the work of the ministry, for the edifying of the body of Christ." What talents has God given you to multiply in serving others while farming the inner city for Christ?

6
Variety in the Garden

"What I like best about working in a Baptist Center," one volunteer commented, "is the enormous variety of people I meet. My experience here has totally changed many of my earlier opinions about what kind of people live in the inner city and the way they respond to the gospel."

This reaction comes not just from one person but from practically every volunteer who ever serves Christ through missions to the inner city. Even when we've known all our lives that every person carries a unique set of fingerprints and biological genes, we still tend to assume all people fit one of our stereotypical molds—until we get to know them better and discover the truth.

Molds never fit anybody. Even people we know very well change constantly as they have new experiences and react in different ways to both their past and present.

Few other types of ministry include such a variety in age, nationality and cultures, level of education, and past experiences and future potential, as well as the way that each responds to the gospel.

Everyone is important to God. At times our human nature tempts us to ignore some and give up on others, but God loves all and invites every living soul to enjoy a personal relationship with him.

Do we comprehend the honor of this special privilege and our responsibility for sharing his love with others?

In the dawn of history "the Lord God formed a man of the dust of the ground, and breathed into his nostrils the breath of life; and man became a living soul" (Gen. 2:7). All people live because God provides their breath of life. All people deserve respect as a product of his handiwork. And all people need to appreciate their source of life and trust the Creator who knows our needs better than we know ourselves.

Since the beginning of time, God has also allowed his human creations the privilege of personal choice. Love never flows by force, only by choice.

But human nature often makes mistakes and chooses destructive ways that God calls sin. But he still refrains from manipulating people like puppets and constantly proves his love, hoping that individuals will love him in return.

In the most extreme effort possible, our Creator proved the depths of his divine love in order to provide our only solution for sin. God himself came in the flesh of Jesus Christ to give us a perfect example for living, paid the price of our sins through the blood he shed dying on the cross, and then proved true our hope of resurrection by rising back to life again. He still lives among us and wants to live within us. His Spirit inhabits the hearts of anyone who invites him in, to forgive his sins and to provide him strength for serving Christ.

Who are we to reject so great a love?

Who are we to shun others who God also loves?

Who are we to know the gospel and refuse to share with others who have not heard and still suffer in their sin?

A Baptist Center in the inner city combines the efforts of many Christians who are grateful for God's love and want to practice doing unto others as they would want others to do unto them if the circumstances were reversed.

Persistence Pays Off

Each person is unique and special unto God. Every person possesses something valuable to contribute to the world.

Appearances, especially in the inner city, can be deceiving.

One excellent example of this is a woman who lived within sight of the Baptist Center in a dilapidated little house where many people would refuse to live.

As one volunteer walked over to take her lunch, curiosity overwhelmed her because recently the newspaper had carried much about the life of this woman. Her immediate family consisted of thirteen dogs, too many cats to count, and a houseful of rats who felt so welcome that they ate—during the same time—from the bowl with the cats. She gave each rat, cat, and dog a special name and respected them simply because they possessed life. In fact, respect for life influenced everything this ninety-year-old woman said and did.

As the volunteer approached the steps, the little lady rose from her porch swing and greeted her with obviously refined diction. Somehow the grimy black sweater, so generously air-conditioned by the rats, just didn't suit the cultured four-and-one-half-foot frame that so hospitably asked the volunteer questions that seemed to invite her friendship.

The conversation ultimately revealed the interesting little lady's extensive education, travels abroad, and a career playing the violin in the Boston Symphony Orchestra. She once enjoyed an elite life of satin and lace, but she had stored many beautiful unworn garments away for "hard times" while her precious rat friends gobbled her piano into a shell and the clothes she wore into rags.

As the volunteer and the little lady discussed the meaning of their names, her bright eyes sparkled as she asked, "How many people do you know with my first name?" It took a minute, but the volunteer mentioned one or two.

Then she said, "Are *they* married?" The reply was no. "See," she chuckled, "I was named after a maiden aunt and it has hindered me ever since. There was one suitor

. . . " her voice trailed off, "but my name chased him away too."

Both the volunteer and the lonely lady enjoyed their visit; but others waited for their lunches further down the street, so they had to say good-bye. But throughout the day the volunteer reflected upon the alertness of the lady despite her age. Some called her brilliant, while others who observed her rats often just raised their eyebrows in suspicion.

But what if she was different or eccentric? Is anyone outside the need for Christ? Doesn't he love the eccentric ones too? Are they not included in both his grace and his command that we teach *all* people about his love?

Besides, who knows what we would do with their set of experiences? The Baptist Center discovered a certain woman from a Christian postman who suggested that someone visit her on the day she had just returned from the hospital after experiencing the trauma of being raped, robbed, and brutally beaten in her own home.

Miss Farmer did go and found her in mortal fear of staying that first night alone at home. The missionary offered to take the little woman home with her, but she said, "No, thank you," quite tenaciously. "It's important that I stay here tonight in order to overcome my fear."

A tour through her house quickly explained those fears. Even when the doors were locked, there were holes in the floor large enough for someone to climb right in. So Miss Farmer recruited some Christian men to patch the holes and install stronger locks on each door. Then the lady, on her own, adopted several more stray dogs to bark at any future intruders.

The city experienced freezing weather in months to come, and the little woman stood too close to her space heater without comprehending how fragile her aging skin had become. Her legs were burned severely.

The doctor wanted to hospitalize her to graft skin across

the burns, but she refused to go. She had fought constantly to keep her dogs and feared that if she remained away from home several days, they would not be there when she returned.

So the doctor instructed Miss Farmer how to care for the burns, and she went daily for weeks on end. Miss Farmer had to be a strong-stomached nurse, but she continued to go.

As the missionary made regular visits, she shared Jesus in many different ways. The lady's reactions included mentioning the special pride she took in the picture of the exquisite lace dress she wore to her childhood confirmation. And she made several superficial statements about "how nice" it was to go to church. But Miss Farmer never judged whether her faith was sincere.

After seventy-eight trips to bathe her burned legs, the bright-eyed little lady looked straight at Miss Farmer and said, "Why do you continue to come? I know of no other living person who would have such patience with me as you do."

As the missionary continued to gently apply the healing salve, she replied, "It's love, my dear. I love you because Jesus loves you."

The spirit of the lady's question made it very natural to continue sharing how she too could have that foundation of real love by receiving the Lord Jesus Christ.

"I do believe," she said.

But this time she attached none of the previous cultural connotations she had nervously added many times before. Now the calm simplicity of her faith was not only beautiful but genuine.

With no prompting, she asked Miss Farmer about the possibility of her being baptized as Jesus was—by immersion. They contacted a pastor concerning this, but her burns never healed enough to make this possible. Yet she continued to mature in her faith.

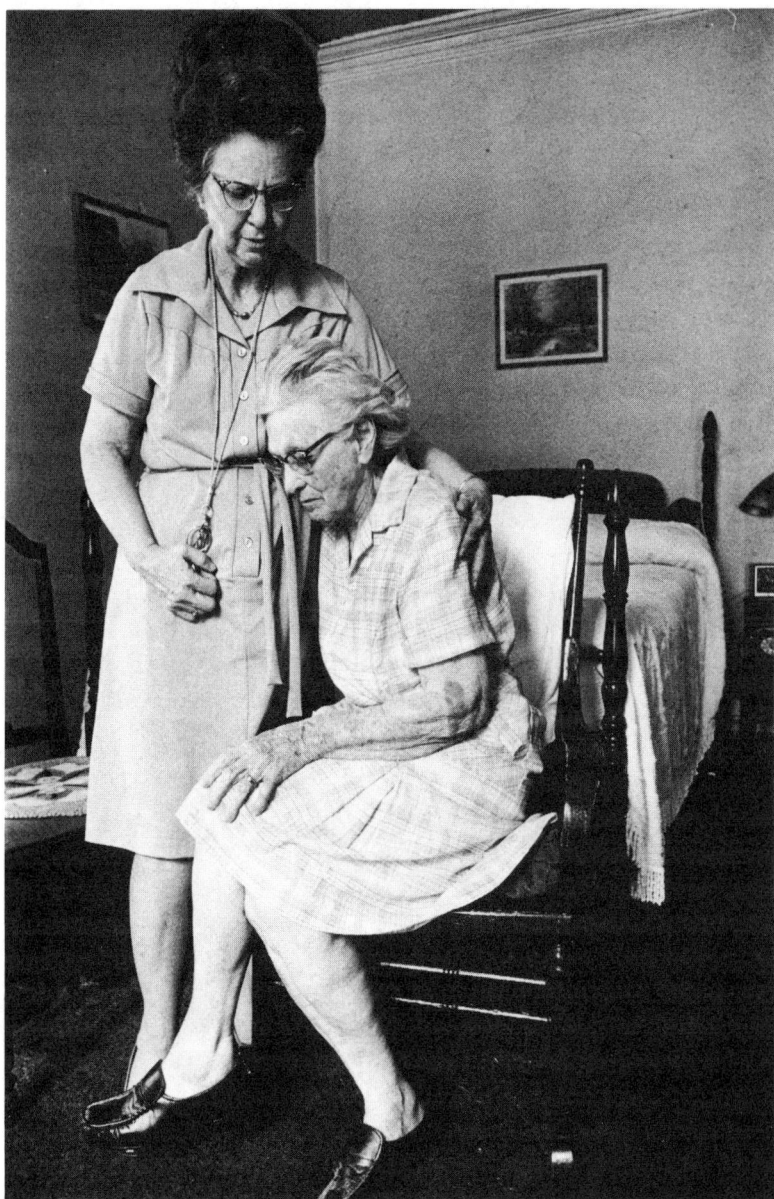

The elderly feel Miss Farmer's compassion and concern in a variety of ways. (Photo by Don Rutledge, Home Mission Board, SBC)

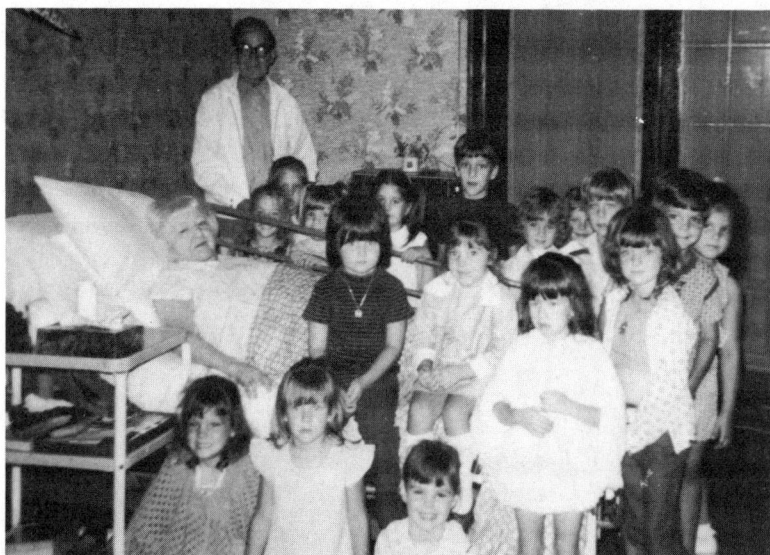

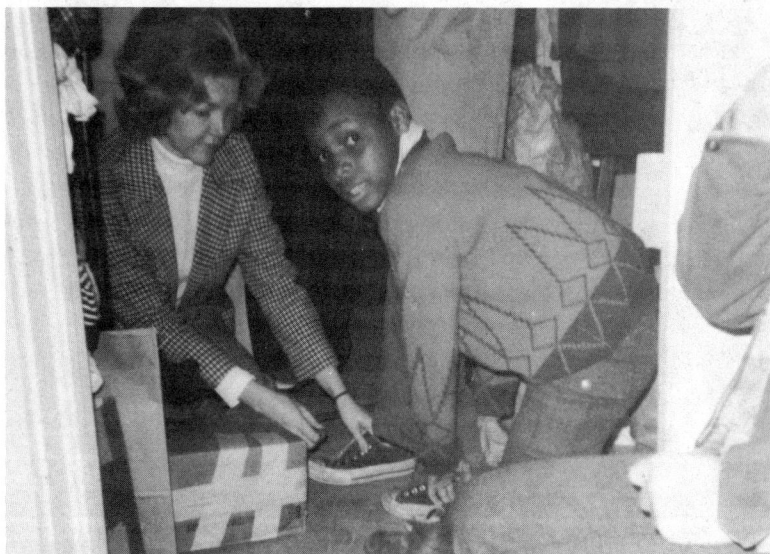

(Upper) This elderly brother greatly appreciated these children lifting the spirits of his shut-in sister with their singing. (Lower) The Baptist Center ministers to all ages and all nationalities, helping with physical, emotional, and spiritual needs.

In the meantime, the Health Department wanted to condemn the lady's unsanitary house. They came to carry its resident to the psychiatric unit of a hospital until a court hearing could take place. As authorities carried the elderly lady away, her best watchdog leaped to her defense and was shot and left bleeding to death unattended.

To a sensitive lady with her full mental capacities, this incident and the sights she soon observed in the psychiatric ward depressed her enormously. As a pampered child she had always gotten her way. As a single adult she knew nothing but freedom without responsibility. But now she was over ninety years old, too frail in body and too set in her ways to change lifetime habits or philosophies.

She could get none of the civil authorities to understand her reasons for living as she did. They just tried to condemn the person along with her property.

Then Gladys Farmer heard what was happening and flew to her defense. She not only strengthened the battered spirit of the woman but marshaled the forces of concerned Christians to make the necessary changes. She also spoke in her behalf at a hearing to get the lady released from a nursing home by promising to help her improve her living environment.

Miss Farmer understood the reasoning of both the Health Department and the elderly lady. But she could also see the possibilities within the situation that many others declared impossible. Too, she knows how to lead others to help her get the job done.

Christian men and women from churches, Community Action, and other agencies responded to the need. With shovels they removed the hardened slime that hid the floors and caused the woman to fall every time it rained through the holes in the roof. They scraped with butcher knives until priceless antiques surfaced from the filth. They patched holes, exterminated, laid linoleum, and painted. Finally her house passed inspection.

Christian love had lifted this woman out of condemnation, and she appreciated every effort.

Several months after returning to her shiny, clean house the little woman died from a series of strokes. After the funeral, one of the relatives that she had tried to ignore for many years called Miss Farmer by phone. "I just wanted to say thank you for the influence you had in the life of my cousin," she said. "We know her heart was changed because several weeks before the strokes began she called every family member she had ever wronged and made things right."

The cousin went on to explain that many years ago another relative had taken a job as a teacher and enjoyed her work very much. But the woman resented the indignity of a cousin disgracing their family by choosing such a "lowly" occupation. She went so far as to request that the school board fire the one she could not persuade to quit. But they refused.

Even though the now-retired teacher had filed that experience far into her past, the little woman brought it back to the surface in order to get her forgiveness.

In order to hide her life-style from relatives, years ago she had threatened to throw acid in the face of anyone who came to visit her. She never told them about any of her problems, even when some tried to call her by phone. After many years they only saw her in person when she was admitted to the nursing home shortly before her death.

A changed heart produced a changed life. Humility replaced pride. Concern replaced selfishness. And nothing but the Spirit of God could have given her the courage to ask forgiveness for inflicting such old wounds.

But what if Miss Farmer and all the volunteers who touched this lady's life had quit after only two or three unsuccessful visits? Instead, they never gave up. Even the eccentric ones are eligible for an eternity in heaven, even though it may require a special and persistent love in ministry. "Let us not be weary in well doing: for in due season we shall reap, if we faint not" (Gal. 6:9).

In Search of Love

While some people are born into advantageous circumstances, others are born disadvantaged and struggle to survive. One lady retells how her mother shot her daddy when she was only two years old. During those years of national depression her mother could not support the little girl and her brother, so she put them in separate Catholic orphanages.

As the youngest of three hundred little girls, she was treated as a substitute "baby doll" instead of getting the genuine love and discipline that she needed. As a preschooler, craving the love of her mother, she once ran away from the orphanage. But the property covered such a large area that after the length of time it took her to walk around its borders, she walked right back in the front door and endured her punishment.

As she entered her teens, her mother remarried and came to take her back home. But she didn't like her new stepfather and ran away again. At the age of thirteen she married a casual acquaintance just to keep from going back home. But, understandably, that marriage failed and she married again later.

With her second husband, she finally felt secure, protected, and genuinely loved. He had grown up in a strong religious home and had served in the military. She leaned heavily upon his faith, self-discipline, and deep love to carry her through many years. Many occasions arose when she needed those qualities inside herself, but no one ever told her how she could obtain them. Through the years her problems multiplied as she drank more and more.

One day as Miss Farmer was inviting some neighborhood children to Family Night, the lady overheard from her chair on the porch. "Hey," she shouted to the missionary, "Just kids! You only like kids don't you? You don't care about us old folks, do you?"

Miss Farmer went over to chat for a while. By the end of the conversation, the lady knew that the Baptist Center helps people of all ages with a spirit of love and concern. Her husband had started riding the van to the Tuesday Family Night, so that night she joined him.

But before leaving she took a secret "swig," thinking no one would ever know. Miss Farmer noticed but never said a word. She treated the lady royally and made her feel welcome enough to want to come back. The Baptist Center gave this woman the first doll she had ever owned and exposed her to Bible truths she had never heard before.

At over seventy years of age she finally received the great love she had so desperately needed—the love of her living heavenly Father. She asked him forgiveness of her sins and invited him in as both Lord and Savior.

Eleven months later tragedy struck. Her beloved husband died and she felt very much alone. Still young in the faith, sometimes she returned to the bottle as an artificial retreat from pain. But Miss Farmer never stopped loving her and came to her bedside at all hours of the day and night to minister her back to health and strengthen her faith so that God could carry her through her grief. Now she's much stronger and doesn't need artificial supports when she can depend on his Spirit.

Many other Christians who have come to know this sweet lady through the Baptist Center have helped her. One brings her books from the library, another takes her to the doctor, and others invite her to their homes for occasional meals.

Everyone loves her outgoing personality and talent for delightfully entertaining conversation. Her cheerfulness lifts the spirits of those who thought they were going there to cheer her up. When one volunteer commented on her jovial nature, she very seriously stated, "I try; but when you're sick all the time and have lost your husband, it's not always easy."

It is important now that she has Christ to provide her strength during the days of loneliness and pain. Only he can give us power equal to all our needs, sweet companionship through the presence of his Holy Spirit and the privilege of prayer.

Lending a Helping Hand

A Baptist Center helps people with a great variety of needs as well as backgrounds. One unmarried Montgomery man had been a Christian for many years, and for quite a while he had shouldered the heavy responsibility of caring for an invalid sister with many complicated problems.

This devoted brother loved his sister without reservation and sacrificially attempted to meet her every need. But depression overwhelmed the invalid, and the brother tried everything to cheer her spirits.

When the Baptist Center first opened he would arrange for someone to sit with her while he went to the fellowship lunches and brought a plate back to his sister.

After Miss Farmer learned of the sister's depression, she tried to visit her many times without success. Then she took this "Southern belle" a meal tray adorned with a lovely magnolia blossom.

This flower opened the door to a beautiful friendship and a wonderful opportunity to minister to many different needs of these genteel people. Many visitors have helped to break the monotony of the sister's long days in bed and her coping with pain. But the love and cheer shared also lightened the heavy responsibility of her brother.

A man of true courtesy and hospitality, he always welcomed guests and graciously thanked them for all they did for his sister. With true generosity he frequently offered volunteers a jar of homemade preserves or a photograph of his sister. He has made contributions to several different churches in gratitude for the mission work of their members. Even while his sister was bedridden, she never failed to send her tithe to be used in the work of the Lord.

Several years after the Baptist Center opened, this lovely, white-haired sister went on to live with the Lord whom she loved. Her death left a great emptiness in the life of her loving brother. Now the Christian friends he has made through the Baptist Center try to strengthen him during this time of adjustment and pray for the Holy Comforter to fill this void with new purpose for his own life.

How sad that many Christians only know the members of their own church family and never meet some of the gems in the soil of the inner city. Missions is a wonderful way to make their acquaintance and to serve Christ at the same time.

Caring for the Children

Matthew 19:14 reads, "But Jesus said, Suffer little children, and forbid them not, to come unto me: for of such is the kingdom of heaven."

In modern language, *suffer* means to *allow* children to come to him. But in a sad irony, far too many children actually do hurt physically and spiritually because of their parents' failure to receive Jesus into their lives.

One set of children fearfully walks the streets while both of their alcoholic parents "fight it out." One night they returned home to find that their daddy had beaten their mother with a sledgehammer, and he was taken to jail.

In another location a mother left her crawling son and toddling daughter at the edge of their grandmother's yard, expecting her to take them in and raise them as her own. She later had a third baby and left it the same way, only this time with a broken arm.

It took many months of patience and loving care to stop one of the fearful babies' persistent crying. But an unmarried epileptic aunt became a wonderful substitute mother and learned quickly through experience how to care for these unwanted children and started bringing them to the Baptist Center as she came for weekly Bible classes. After several weeks, volunteers in the nursery told Miss Farmer about a need they didn't know how to handle. The children's clothes contained particles of feces that indicated that someone washed diapers with outer garments without rinsing the dirty diapers first. In the interest of the children's health, they felt something had to be said before the children got sick. So they asked the missionary if she would mind doing so.

The missionary thanked them for bringing this to her attention and said she would try to find a way to help. So as the van took the ladies and their children home, Miss Farmer arranged to sit in the back beside the one who brought the children and mentioned the concern of the volunteers.

In a gracious and tactful way she exposed the problem, assuring the lady that she too would not have known how to wash diapers if her mother had not taught her how. But she just wanted to help in whatever way she could because she recognized that this unmarried aunt was showing such sacrificial love to these children. She recognized that it must surely take special courage to handle such active tots, still squirming in her arms.

The woman greatly appreciated this practical advice she had never known before. She thanked the missionary for bringing it to her attention and said she would certainly take her suggestion. The next week when she returned, she showed Miss Farmer what a wonderful improvement her suggestion had made in her wash.

These tots have now matured into beautiful, healthy, well-adjusted children who love Jesus and are growing in their faith. But through this we can see the diversity of needs in missions. These concerned Christians didn't just shake their heads and turn the other way. They saw a need and ministered to the glory of the Lord. Now these children will be more acceptable to society as well as enjoying better health.

Many of the adults who come to Baptist Centers have already experienced broken lives. But the teaching of children with a potential for many social handicaps opens possibilities that ought to excite us into action.

As one teacher showed the pictures of some community helpers, she asked the children what they thought they might like to become one day. A few offered the typical answers of doctor, lawyer, teacher, and policeman.

But one said, "I wanna steal like Quincy." (He was referring to the man his mother allowed to sleep in their home when he wasn't out gathering "surprises" to bring back in a bedsheet to display before the eyes of the impressionable children.)

If only the children of the inner city could be more strongly influenced by the goodness of God than the badness of the world! Please make this your prayer.

Missions to the inner city touches a variety of needs and gets a variety of responses. But they all require the same solution, Jesus Christ, and it takes a variety of Christians with many different talents to lead them to the Lord who loves us all.

7
Sowing the Seed

"There was a man who went out to sow grain. As he scattered the seed in the field, some of it fell along the path, and the birds came and ate it up. Some of it fell on rocky ground, where there was little soil. The seeds soon sprouted, because the soil wasn't deep. When the sun came up, it burned the young plants; and because the roots had not grown deep enough, the plants soon dried up. Some of the seed fell among thorn bushes, which grew up and choked the plants. But some seeds fell in good soil, and the plants bore grain: some had one hundred grains, others sixty, and others thirty" (Matt. 13:3–8, TEV).

Reading the parable of the sower is like walking into a training session for laborers in God's field, conducted by the greatest farmer of all—Jesus Christ the Lord.

Baptist Centers and other phases of Christian social ministry frequently give wonderful orientations for volunteers eager to serve God through missions. But the parable of the sower is probably the most concise and timeless teaching available. It prepares Christians to expect many different reactions to their witness and shows that even the field of one heart can respond to seeds of the gospel in several different ways.

Hear more of Jesus' seminar: "Those who hear the message about the Kingdom but do not understand it are like the seeds that fell along the path. The Evil One comes and snatches away what was sown in them. The seeds that fell on rocky ground stand for those who receive the message gladly as soon as they hear it. But it does not sink deep in them, and they don't last long. So when trouble or persecution comes because of the message, they give up at once. The seeds that fell among thorn bushes stand for those who hear the message; but the worries about this life and the love for riches choke the message, and they don't bear fruit. And the seed sown in the good soil stands for those who hear the message and understand it: they bear fruit, some as much as one hundred, others sixty, and others thirty" (Matt. 13:19–23, TEV).

Jesus flatly stated that some people can both see and hear his teachings without really letting those truths sink deep enough into their souls to ever make a difference in their lives. But blessed are they who spiritually see and hear because when they do, God promises to multiply their comprehension.

Jesus explained his symbolism for the seed in Matthew 13:38 by saying that "the good seed are the children of the kingdom" and in Luke 8:11 by saying that "The seed is the word of God." There's no discrepancy in this because it can be both at the same time. Planting of the seed occurs as Christians share the Word of God.

He explains other equivalents as well. "He that soweth the good seed is the Son of man" (Matt. 13:37). Jesus does the sowing. He scatters Christians across the world, expecting them to share the Word. Witnessing is not optional for believers. As his seed, our purpose is to produce growth through sharing the Word of God.

Some people hesitate to share out of fear that they will encounter rejection or not know how to handle an acceptance. But Jesus deals with that uncertainty by telling us to expect different reactions. There will be some rejections. Some ground is too hard to absorb the gospel, but that should never stop us from sharing. Predators of the gospel promise to gobble up hope, but that should never stop us from praying.

On other occasions the Word of God will be absorbed and grow a little. But shallow soil on a rocky foundation will cause some growth to wither in the heat of persecution.

Some hearts receive God's Word and try to grow, but the distractions of daily living and concern about money sometimes choke young growth long before maturity.

Yet no seed sown for Christ falls in vain. If we sow without ceasing, Jesus' parable also promises that some seeds will produce multiple success, one hundred times, sixty times or thirty times! And these results make every effort worthwhile.

All that we say about the total field of the world can equally apply to individuals, even to our own spiritual growth. One heart may sometimes refuse to absorb some Scriptures and then grow a bit with others before withering in the heat of persecution. Sometimes we allow figurative weeds to choke our spiritual maturity. But if we consistently sow the seed of God's Word, some soil will eventually reproduce spiritual fruit, one hundred, sixty, or thirty times. And that makes patience priceless!

Encountering Stony Ground

The sight of the man's face and hands immediately told volunteers that he had been terribly burned. When they asked if they could have a blessing with him for the food they had brought, he put a mechanical amplifier up to the hole in his throat and refused to allow them to pray. They heard later that he had undergone surgery for cancer that had threatened his life and now prevented normal speech.

Most people would assume that such extreme circumstances would cause a person to lean upon the Lord, but instead he refused to believe in God. He disagreed with the moral teachings of Jesus and chose to trust only himself.

Jesus said we can expect to encounter some stony ground. But spiritual hardness involves more than those who boastfully call themselves atheists. The seed also lies exposed on the surface of all hearts who reject God's truth.

Pray for God's Spirit to soften the soil so that people will invite the seed to take root in their hearts.

In addition to spiritual hardness, missionaries and volunteers farming the inner city for Christ also encounter stony physical areas that are enormously difficult to deal with. Alcoholism, drug addiction, sexual perversion, and mental illness try the patience of all who minister in love. Scores of persons with these characteristics show slow or no improvement, but missionary Gladys Farmer patiently persists among many, hoping that at least a few will be saved.

One day during an unusual calm at the Baptist Center a knock came at the door. Miss Farmer greeted the lady who was leaning on a walking stick. She knew her very well. After nursing her through many times of sickness in her home, the missionary had sacrificially helped her through several personal crises in a spirit of genuine friendship.

The lady had accepted Christ months ago, but now she needed professional help for mental illness. Yet she had no family to recognize this and was too sick to admit it herself. After they talked in the hall awhile, the woman started accusing the missionary of robbing a bank and proceeded to beat her with the heavy walking stick.

Miss Farmer immediately recognized this as another manifestation of the mental illness for which the Baptist Center had tried to help the woman see a need for treatment many times before, but she had refused.

It often takes a long time to get treatment involuntarily. The law that protects the civil rights of many mental patients often slows down assistance for others. The criteria for getting treatment when people are too sick to ask voluntarily requires:

1. Proof that the person is mentally ill
2. Proof that the person is dangerous to himself or others

3. Proof that this danger has been evidenced by a recent overt action

4. That the treatment they need is presently available

5. That the least restrictive setting be selected for adequate care. (If a person can get the help he needs on an outpatient basis, then that is preferred over an institution.) Even after dismissal, medical personnel usually suggest that the patient have periodic checkups, but the individual maintains the freedom to follow through.

During their physical struggle, Miss Farmer learned that even elderly mental patients can be exceedingly strong. She tried with all her might to protect herself without hurting the sick woman.

"I love you, I love you," she shouted, trying to calm the raging spirit. "I love you, honey, please relax," she prayerfully pleaded as the angry woman tore the missionary's hairstyle into disheveled disarray.

But during this time, another inner-city resident was using the Baptist Center's washer and dryer in the laundry nook upstairs. After investigating the frightening commotion, she immediately ran to the phone and called for help.

Later, still trembling after authorities took the sick woman away, Miss Farmer cried out to God, "Oh Lord, why must it go so far before we can get these people some help?"

She referred not only to this one who could now be proven "dangerous to themselves and to others" but to the countless others who walk the streets daily, endangered, but too sick to see their need until there's a catastrophe.

Many other incidents involving the mentally ill have consumed more of this missionary's time than anyone but God will ever know. She has ministered like a long-suffering mother to a host of undisciplined and mentally disturbed children in adult bodies. "But who will help them if Christians don't?" she says.

Mental health authorities balance on a tightrope, trying to protect the rights of some without infringing on the rights of others. In fact, the same law that has slowed down help for many has mercifully freed countless others who might have been committed to institutions incorrectly years ago.

Social problems such as these are hard ground on which to minister either physically or spiritually. And often it seems that most seeds of progress eventually are snatched away.

Shallow Ground *vs.* the Sun

Some new believers in the inner city suffer for their faith more than many realize. Unlike communities where everyone usually rejoices when a loved one is saved, in the inner city sometimes Christians meet icy stares from people who wonder if this will now make them judgmental of others' sins or divide their friendship. Discouragement and abuse often threaten the shallow roots of new growth.

When one crippled woman gave her heart to Jesus, she vowed to make a clean break with her life of adultery. But when she boldly explained her decision to the man in her life, he became enraged and put a padlock on her door that permitted only him to go and come as he wished.

Concerned Christians discovered this while trying to take a meal to the lady, but she fearfully begged them to leave lest he find them there and vent his wrath on them as well. Fearing that their involvement would endanger her safety, they waited prayerfully and cautiously, considering the right course of action in line with her request.

Unfortunately the situation grew worse immediately. They saw a notice of her death in the newspaper and learned later that she had been beaten to death and lain across a heater. But no charges were pressed.

"Oh God, if only this could have been prevented! Help us know your will sooner before such tragedies occur." This is the prayer and purpose of the Baptist Center staff who grieve in love and work in faith in order to share the truth that could prevent deaths both now and forever. Christ is our only hope for a livable world today and a continuing life tomorrow.

Sometimes new Christians have to count the cost daily when they decide to follow Jesus. Without prompting from anyone but the Holy Spirit, one widowed mother grew dissatisfied with her dependence upon a monthly welfare check when she was really able to work. Even though limited in education, she found a semiskilled job that provided the basic necessities for herself and her son but nothing for luxuries or contingencies.

Forfeiting her previous Medicaid benefits became a real venture in faith. But even when she couldn't see the solution in advance, God always provided for her needs at the right time.

Other heat that threatens shallow growth sometimes comes in the form of cults that profess someone other than Jesus of Nazareth. They often take advantage of people not yet strong in their faith, people who have at least opened their minds to spiritual teachings. This new eagerness to listen decreases a cult's labor in new member cultivation as well as makes an immature believer vulnerable to words that promise love.

The cults frequently test the genuine commitment and dedication of witnessing Christians. Teachers in one of a housing project's Bible studies had a scare one day when leaders of one of the robed cults stood watching the activities of the Bible study. When the children were dismissed, cult leaders threw candy in the air and whispered in the ears of students who ran to pick it up.

Montgomery had just experienced a confrontation between police and cult leaders who had temporarily taken over a local radio station. So the Baptist Center and the director of the housing project agreed that they should discontinue the group Bible studies until the tension eased.

Fortunately their prayers were answered when this particular cult moved on to another city. The Baptist Center was invited to resume classes in that same housing project.

Satanic threats pose a reality that Christians must recognize and work through while the doors remain open. From one day to the next we never know when that opportunity may cease. When farming souls for Christ we must recognize all predators—weeds, weather conditions, soil variations—all in order to reap the harvest that God promises if we faithfully labor.

One black lady said, "I don't have transportation to a church. But I'll listen to anybody who comes to our neighborhood. For a while the Mormons went from door to door and I read their books. I liked the Pentecostal preacher who sang hymns while walking up and down the street too, but he stopped coming. The Black Muslims seemed like just another group, so I listened to them, too. But nobody seems to come long enough to make me feel solid about anything."

This woman's comment is typical of many who would be glad to hear the gospel if someone cared enough to share. The church often overlooks such fertile soil thirsting for spiritual nourishment and continually reworks much tired ground while hungry souls die and go to hell.

Faith Threatened by Thorns

One of the most common varieties of thorns that choke the sharing of the gospel is fear of unknown situations, of different nationalities, of not knowing what to say, of wondering what to do. Sometimes those fears only indicate a shallowness of faith. Satan uses the thorns of fear to the maximum in order to choke missions in every way possible.

Despite countless experiences most people might consider potentially fearful, Gladys Farmer testifies that God has always protected her. She states plainly, "There can be no safer place than the center of God's will. If I stayed away from somewhere that I really felt the Lord was urging me to go—*then* I would be in danger."

When one terminally ill black lady called Miss Farmer to say she had no food and was very hungry, the missionary didn't consider what time of night it was or that even the police hesitated to go to that particular neighborhood after dark. She simply went. The lady had trusted her, so she trusted the heavenly Father's protection.

She thought she would recognize the right apartment, but driving through the neighborhood at night made the brick buildings look more alike than ever. Very few porch lights were on, so she had great difficulty seeing house numbers. Unsure of just what to do, she prayed for God's help to find the right address.

Across the way, a large group of older black boys were gathered and playing basketball. She drove up to them, rolled down her car window, and asked if anyone could tell her how she could find the apartment of the sick lady who needed food.

After a moment of silence one said, "Is that you, Miss Farmer?"

"Why, yes," she replied, a bit surprised that someone recognized her in the dark. "And who are you?" she asked.

He introduced himself as a student of one of the mission Vacation Bible Schools several years ago and reminded the others of who she was. They asked what she was doing in their neighborhood at this hour, and she explained her inability to find the address of the sick woman who had asked for some food.

"Come on, Miss Farmer," the young man said, "we'll escort you right to her door." When she got out of her car they formed a circle around her and walked her straight to the apartment, waited outside while she visited with the sick lady, and then walked her back to the car when she finished her visit. She had never felt so well protected in her life—by God and people.

They welcomed her because she had come to them first sharing God's Word in love. If we hope to live in a world without fear, we too must take the initiative and share in love or accept the results of our own refusal to go.

Once as Miss Farmer and some volunteers passed out leaflets from door to door in a community known for its delinquency, she heard a booming voice out of nowhere yell, "Old white lady!"

She stood very still and looked to see where the volunteers were, since she felt responsible for them. But they moved about happily in other places, so she felt they were safe.

So she just prayerfully skipped the next apartment and continued sharing leaflets at each door thereafter. Such peace flooded her soul that she had to put a brochure across her lips to suppress a chuckle as she prayed, "Well, Lord, at least he called me a lady."

Satan wants us to fear. He wants us to turn around and run. He tempts us with anything that will snatch away the seed of the gospel from all who need to hear.

But Gladys Farmer trusted God's protection, and so did those volunteers. As a result of their faith, many children attended Vacation Bible School, heard the gospel, and invited Christ into their lives as both Lord and Savior. Now we trust that that decision will multiply so others will have no reason to fear them in the future.

If the early Christians had feared persecution enough to be silent, the gospel would never have reached our generation today. Should we do any less for those who live after us?

Pray seriously that more Christians will grow deep enough in their faith to say with the apostle Paul, "Nevertheless I am not ashamed: for I know whom I have believed, and am persuaded that he is able to keep that which I have committed unto him against that day" (2 Tim. 1:12).

Thorns that Choke Growth

The concentrated population of the inner city represents a tangle of many different choking weeds. Few families are fortunate enough to have only one problem. Weeds in the inner city come in bunches, with an amazing capacity to multiply.

New believers living in city jungles often try to grow in their faith despite an abundance of choking thorns such as alcoholism, drugs, illiteracy, adultery, and prostitution, sometimes coping with mental or physical handicaps, unemployment or low wages, undesirable housing and discouraging friends, constant bedlam, and utter frustration.

I wish we could say that all grow stronger despite such experiences, but unfortunately such tangles choke the life of some. One struggle involved a beautiful strawberry-blonde twelve-year-old who loved Jesus with all her heart. A glow came over this precious retarded girl's face as she sang "I Have Decided to Follow Jesus" at the Baptist Center on Family Night.

But taking her back home to the bedlam was almost like casting a lamb to the wolves. She begged her family to attend the church where she had joined, but no one would. Her father was an alcoholic, her mother a shy illiterate.

As long as they lived in this neighborhood this beautiful little girl, her sister, and a brother caught the van to attend classes to Family Night. Later the family moved to a cleaner neighborhood, yet many of their habits and problems remained the same.

Eventually the distance involved caused the Baptist Center to lose contact with them until several years later when they heard the young believer's name related in a news report. Hunters had found the now seventeen-year-old girl shot in the head and lying among the weeds.

Her family and friends never knew who killed her or why. But through this experience the young girl had left her witness. Her mother was saved, and two other family members were drawn closer to the Lord as the caring missionary ministered to them during this time of grief with the same sweet spirit she did in strengthening them against the thorns.

Sometimes people who live in sheltered suburbia try to ignore the certainty of death. But the people of the inner city are faced with death almost every day. The reality of death requires urgency in farming the inner city for Christ.

Seed that Multiplies

Second Corinthians 9:6 promises, "But this I say, He which soweth sparingly shall reap also sparingly; and he which soweth bountifully shall reap also bountifully."

The entire effort of missions often requires the sowing of many seeds before results are harvested, but with ceaseless sowing some will be won. God doesn't promise that labor in his field will be easy. Missions requires faith, demands time, needs patience, is often watered with tears, must be motivated by commitment, and grows only by the power of the Holy Spirit.

Faithful laborers who farm the inner city for Christ sometimes never even see the multiplication of the seed they've sown and could easily be discouraged with the slowness of growth. This is especially true in working with transients, when only about one in six hundred shows a sincere interest in receiving Jesus as his personal Savior. A wanderer's focus is usually just on his immediate physical needs such as hunger, clothing, and a place to sleep. Most have nowhere to go—they're just going.

Sometimes the multiplication of the seed takes place even

after the people have moved to another location, where God uses another servant to reap the harvest that required a long time to grow.

But the greatest joy of living, and certainly the greatest joy in missions, comes at that moment when someone says, "Now I'm ready. I want Jesus in my life."

The ones who also become soul-winners are exceptional among the converts in the inner city and are more often found among the teenagers. One Sunday afternoon Miss Farmer was taking a sack of groceries to a couple when two French children flagged her down on Perry Street.

"Miss Farmer, my mother believed in Jesus Christ before she died," George shouted with joy as the missionary stopped her car.

It had been quite a while since she had seen these young friends. Their parents had separated, and the mother moved them quite a distance to the country where she could be with relatives after she was stricken with cancer. She later died, and the children were now visiting in Montgomery.

"I told her everything I could remember about Jesus, and she trusted him to save her," George said. Then his sister Veleta added, "I feel sure she had turned her life to Jesus, Miss Farmer, and we thank him for saving her."

Even from different cities where Miss Farmer served years ago, people still call or write to say that the seed sown in their hearts along the way has bloomed both in their lives and in the lives of others.

The challenge is great! God promised eventual success. And no harvest comes without planting the seed. We live among an abundance of weeds, and Satan promises to sow more. But much of the field still waits and is ready for harvest.

8
Reflection at Sunset

Hardworking laborers deserve a time of relaxation, reflection, philosophizing, and the joy of admiring the fruit that has matured from seed they helped to sow. When workers in God's field are privileged to see spiritual seeds mature, that reward seems like a tiny foretaste of heaven.

After a twenty-eight-year absence, Missionary Gladys Farmer returned to the island of Kauai where she first served as a foreign missionary and savored the joy of observing God's handiwork in the lives of many who were saved during her appointment there.

This rare opportunity came as a collective gift from many loving people in the Montgomery Baptist Association to celebrate Miss Farmer's sixty-fourth birthday on February 14, 1978.

The idea originated as Mrs. Betty Reeves, one of the teachers at the Riverside Heights Bible study, prayed in private for a way to go to the Holy Land. During this prayer she felt that the Lord was saying, "Why not Gladys Farmer instead?"

Betty smiled and replied, "Lord, I was praying for myself; but if you want Miss Farmer to go I'll be glad to do whatever I can to make it possible."

So the next time Betty saw the missionary, she commented that she believed the Lord wanted Miss Farmer to go to the Holy Land instead of herself. Miss Farmer was shocked.

The director of the Baptist Center explained that she

was much too busy with plans for the mission Vacation Bible Schools and a heavy schedule of speaking engagements during the annual emphasis on home missions to afford the luxury of time off for a trip to the Holy Land.

"Anyway, if I ever go anywhere, I prefer it to be in order to work for the Lord instead of for personal pleasure," she replied in humility. Still mulling it over, she added pensively, "But if I ever had the choice, I would probably return to see the people of Hawaii where I first served as a foreign missionary."

Betty smiled and dropped the subject. But secretly she began to invite WMU ladies around the city to share in supplying a plane ticket to Hawaii for Miss Farmer's sixty-fourth birthday celebration.

The occasion happened to fall on Tuesday, which includes a busy Family Night at the Baptist Center. The cheerful conspirators asked Brother and Mrs. Boyd to call Miss Farmer downstairs to discuss something in the youth Bible study. This enabled the WMU ladies and guests to prepare the tables in the chapel so that everyone who attended Family Night could share in the celebration.

The teachers knew to bring everyone in at a specified time. And the children couldn't have behaved more beautifully. The entire atmosphere seemed to overflow with love.

As always, the surprised Miss Farmer struggled inwardly with her reluctance to receive. It's so much easier for her to give. But she graciously swallowed her pride as Mrs. Reeves presented her with the ticket and some money for extra expenses. She consented to take the trip "just because of the love it represented on the part of so many people who helped to make it possible."

Then she added, "Even though I have often wished to go back to see the people of Hawaii, I never expected to have the opportunity—unless perhaps the Lord chose to pull back the curtain a bit and show me a little glimpse on my way to heaven. But I do greatly appreciate what each of you have done to give me this little taste of heaven during my time on earth."

Just a Bit of Heaven

Miss Farmer's many commitments to speaking engagements delayed her leaving until the middle of April, but she finally left to revisit her first field of service. Mrs. Aylene Wiggins, a long-time friend from Enoree, South Carolina, met her in Atlanta to join her on the trip.

For three days they thought they would have to stay in Honolulu because the heavy tourist trade complicated hotel accommodations in Kauai. But the people of the Waimea Baptist Church telegrammed her to come on to the island of Kauai and stay in the pastorium that was now vacant; they were awaiting the arrival of a new pastor in a few weeks. The joy of staying in the same mission home where she had lived so long ago brought back precious memories that far outweighed any luxurious hotel suite.

And these people without a pastor also fulfilled her earlier statement about wanting to serve wherever she went. They asked her to help them in visitation and to speak in both church services. During the Sunday School hour she shared with the Japanese members of their congregation with the help of Mrs. Hayruo Masaki, the same faithful bilingual translator who had assisted her in 1948.

"Few joys on earth can compare to this privilege of seeing people who were saved over twenty years ago and are now mature in the Lord and enthusiastically sharing what he means in their lives and in the lives of others they've been privileged to win," she confided to the people of Waimea on Sunday. And she added with a heart full of compassion, "This is what I pray for for the people back home as well."

In the stillness of the night she was too absorbed with reflections on God's work over the past years to go right to sleep. She recalled the experience with amoeba that forced her to leave these lovely people. But despite that

The staff—Miss Farmer, Bob Franklin, and Milton Boyd—plan together on all aspects of Christian social ministries.

sickness, she praised God for transplanting her to an area where she could serve more people in one city than lived on this entire island.

Through that and the rheumatoid arthritis God taught her a valuable lesson in empathy—how to understand the hurts of others enough that she could share and help lift the weight of their burdens. And what a variety of hurts people endure, both in the Paradise of the Pacific and in the poverty in the inner city! But even more wonderful are the ways God can heal those hurts!

During their stay in Hawaii, the gracious hostesses took their guests on sight-seeing tours of many places that Miss Farmer never visited while serving in missions there. One tour included a memorial to the men who lost their lives during World War II battles in the Pacific. This brought back many frightening recollections of the past, but it also made her impatient to even more boldly witness to the living dead who still walk the streets of our cities.

This return visit to Hawaii gave her a greater appreciation for that earlier appointment as well as additional assurance that she still serves within God's will even in a different location. Both she and Mrs. Wiggins were reluctant to leave these gracious people, but their time of reflection soon ended. This time of physical relaxation and spiritual saturation energized them both and renewed their desire to now work even harder for the Lord who had enabled them to enjoy the beauties of his harvest in Hawaii.

Greetings and Advice

A relaxing time of reflection is also an appropriate time for giving advice. And that's part of a missionary's job too. When Miss Farmer returned to the Baptist Center after completing her vacation in Hawaii, she was greeted with a mountain of birthday cards and letters that had continued to pour in while she was away, which needed to be answered.

Several missions magazines list the names of missionaries and their birthday. Many people use this information in prayer and often send lovely birthday cards or write personal letters individually or collectively as a mission group.

The Baptist Center gets between five hundred and one thousand letters each year from people interested in missions. Miss Farmer tries very hard to answer each request.

To one who loves her Lord so much and thoroughly enjoys her work, it is quite natural for Gladys Farmer to encourage others to experience the joys of missions.

The following are excerpts of some of the letters she receives:

DEAR MISS FARMER,

"I have been reading about you in my *Discovery*. How does it feel to be a missionary?"

"How do you get people to listen while you tell them about Jesus?"

"I was sort of surprised to learn there are poor people— and lost—in the state of Alabama."

"I was twelve when I was saved. Ever since that time I have always wanted to be a missionary. I love telling people about God and how wonderful he is. I was just wondering if you could give me some helpful hints about mission work."

The delightful letters the Baptist Center receives are too numerous to reprint. But God sees the caring hearts of all who express such interest in missions.

In offering advice to young people who think God might be calling them into full-time service through missions, she frequently includes the following suggestions:

1. Find a quiet place and talk with God. When you think the Lord is leading you in this direction, pray. It doesn't have to be a fancy prayer—just one that comes straight

from your heart. The following sample might help you get started: "Dear Father, teach me to understand what I am experiencing. I would rather please you with my life than anything I know. I offer my life to both follow and serve you, dear Lord. In Jesus' name, amen."

2. Write to the personnel departments of the Foreign and Home Mission Boards requesting information concerning requirement, training, age, etc., for missionary appointment.

3. You may want to share your feelings or experience with your pastor, Sunday School teacher, parents, or a friend.

4. Seek and look for God's will as you read your Bible and spend time in prayer.

5. Live daily for Jesus. This involves sharing your faith with others—all nationalities, rich or poor, anyone without Jesus.

To those who ask her to briefly summarize her total philosophy of life and work as a missionary, she replies:

"Every Christian is privileged of our Lord to be a witness—to share his or her faith with a lost, undone world! What a privilege! 'I'm a child of the King' becomes our theme, and involvement in missions becomes a challenge, a joy—not just something to check on a chart!

"The very thought that Jesus would *call me* to serve in his work becomes more exciting every day of my life! The joy of the Lord is my strength!

"The job for Jesus is big—the crime, the sin, the problems and heartbreaks of people who do not know Jesus is enough to blow one's mind! *But his strength and grace enables us to share God's love and forgiveness—to shine like lights in a dark place!*"

Encouraging New Ministries

From time to time other letters arrive saying, "We want to start a weekday ministry in our community (city). Any advice you might be able to offer would be greatly appreciated."

We hope much of the experiences already cited in other chapters will prove helpful to those considering opening such a work, but perhaps we could summarize some of the basics:

1. *Determine the city's needs.*—The Strategy Planning Program outlined by the Home Mission Board has been extremely helpful in reassessing our progress and needs after seven years of experience. But it would be equally beneficial to those considering opening a new work.

It helps to tailor plans to the special needs of your own city instead of copying a different environment. As the Home Mission Board says, "The only way Baptist Centers are alike is that they're different."

Once you clearly see the needs, you can pray more specifically and work more efficiently.

2. *Recognize Christian resources.*—Reaching a city depends upon its size and needs. It can be done by local people alone or with a missionary leading local people, by one church or an entire association. Larger cities in particular need a missionary to take the initiative in planning and then to guide the implementation of those plans. When a missionary is invited, the Home Mission Board must be consulted regarding that transfer.

Someone has to lead out in starting such a ministry and supporting an adequate budget. Rev. J. Frank Hixon laid the wonderful groundwork for the missions that continue to grow in Montgomery, but many supportive pastors contributed important efforts in countless other ways.

Missions is the church at work in the world. And the continuing support of local pastors and volunteers is essential. Without either, a missionary would be severely handicapped.

3. *Survey secular social agencies.*—A good rapport with other agencies helps in many different ways. The partial

list in "Neighbors Along the Road" on page 149–150 will vary from city to city. But many similar organizations will probably offer comparable services. Just remember, a Christian social ministry is different only as it offers Christ in addition to physical help. Teach for prevention as well as for cure.

4. *Pray—pray—pray.*—God must start this work, remain the central focus, and supply the growth. Without him, all things would be impossible. With him, caring Christians can reach their city for Christ.

5. *Select the site and plan the work.*—Most of what needs to be considered here has already been discussed in "Purchasing the Land" and "Preparing the Ground." See chapters 3 and 4 for accounts of Montgomery's experiences.

6. *Communicate with the people.*—Messages can reach the people through hand-delivered leaflets, individual mailings, an associational paper, the state Baptist paper, or as word is passed through key leaders such as pastors, WMU leaders, committee leaders, or others. Keep an up-to-date file of important people for communication. Photos and posters also help. Share in churches as invited. People respond when they have the proper information.

Try to fit the abilities of volunteers to areas for which they are best suited. The Montgomery Baptist Center uses the following checklist so volunteers can state their preferences:

SON-shine Coffeehouse
Receptionist: phone, door
Case load, people in need
Teach Bible to adults, youth, or children
Assist with tour groups
Lead group singing
Sort and share clothing
Type letters, reports, etc.
Repair equipment

Art to kids (spot talent)
Outings, picnics, trips
Enlist other volunteers
Help trouble-prone youth
Carpenter, painter
Teach crafts to kids, adults
Make posters—promote needs
Drama—Bible lessons, etc.
Lead discussions on SSI, family, health, agencies
Tutoring
Driver of van
Literacy teacher
Transportation to clinic, etc.
Work groups—many jobs
Mark Bibles with "Plan of Salvation"
Mend special garments
Check on shut-ins by phone
Play musical instrument
Tell character stories
Learn routes to carry meals
Adopt a shut-in
Others

So much more could be said to advise new ministries, but at least this might give you some idea of where to start. Of course the more needs we help, the more needs we uncover. But the joys always outweigh the problems for Christians willing to farm their inner city for Christ.

Planning for Tomorrow

As autumn exploded with color, Gladys Farmer reflectively compared the trees to the beautiful maturing of all areas of Christian social ministries by the Montgomery Baptist Association. Organizations benefit from a leader's time of reflection to reexamine priorities and plan properly for an increasingly effective ministry.

After the retirement of Reverend J. Frank Hixon, their dedicated leader for twenty years, the Montgomery Baptist Association called Bob Lee Franklin as the new director of associational missions. Mrs. Mae Karn, their equally dedicated secretary for thirty years, had retired a few months before Brother Hixon; and Mrs. Belva Tarleton filled her position. So by March 1977 this all-new staff in the associational office set to work on many new ideas for Christian social ministries, of which the Baptist Center is only one phase.

Among his first priorities, the energetic Mr. Franklin wanted to get a total view of what the association was presently doing in order to define the challenges of the future. So he recommended that they enter into the Home Mission Board's program of strategy planning.

For one year, under the chairmanship of Colonel Charles Todd, various subcommittees conducted a detailed study of a total view of the city's needs. They surveyed the movement of the city's population in order to predict future church sites. They studied church data and evaluated the associational program's parallel with the trend of the people. They researched police statistics and court activities, as well as many community welfare and social service agencies—all to see what the association of forty-six churches could more effectively do to reach people for Christ.

The challenges that this study identified included the following that might give other cities some ideas:

1. Minister to troubled youth
2. Coordinate city/county jail ministries
3. Establish an expanded campus ministry for local colleges
4. Purchase site locations for new churches in areas where high population growth is expected
5. Become aware of community social services
6. Begin truck-stop ministry

7. Establish a church at the Baptist Center to nurture converts

8. Minister to singles and singles again

9. Extend ministry to nursing homes with youth involvement

10. Provide leadership in the association on the black/white issue and establish churches in predominantly black areas which have no churches.

Other recommendations dealt specifically with the promotion of the association. Montgomery Baptists have learned that churches working together benefit individually and collectively as they cooperate in educational programs and leadership training, in discussion and decision making on matters that affect the entire city, and in everyone's involvement in missions to people of the city who aren't affiliated with any church.

Concerned Christians responded immediately to the strategy planning goals that were adopted at the annual associational meeting in October 1978, so Mr. Franklin enthusiastically began implementation.

Within the first five months after the adoption of these goals, several programs bloomed immediately. Members of First Baptist Church jumped at the opportunity to lead in worship services at the Baptist Center on Sunday, while volunteers from all over the city prepared well to teach conversational English to internationals in a Christian atmosphere.

Even though volunteers were once discouraged from visiting in the prisons, God has now opened the doors wide to several institutions.

Youthful offenders approaching parole visit the outside world several times under supervision before their actual release. The relaxed Christian atmosphere of the SONshine Coffeehouse appealed to the warden, who was having difficulty in finding appropriate opportunities for such outings; and the Christians were happy for the opportunity to witness.

Christian counselors have trained in many special orientations in order to know how to help these youth. They pray that this ministry will be effective in helping them return to society as new people, with Christ motivating their lives.

In order to improve communication between the association and the churches, the pastors were asked to select laypersons from each congregation to serve on a Volunteers in Missions (VIM) committee that discusses the needs and goals of the association and then share them with their home church. This gets more laymen involved and relieves some of the heavy responsibilities of their pastor.

So many challenges lie ahead that it seems as if the work has just begun. But God has blessed it richly with some of the following results:

• Inactive Christians have started practicing missions.
• Many people have received Christ as their personal Savior—1,033 professions of faith over a seven-year period.
• Many desperate needs have been met.
• Missions no longer sounds far away to Montgomerians.
• Churches have grown closer as members share together in labor.
• Busy members of one congregation experience the joy of working with dedicated Christians from other churches as they meet in ministering to the inner city.
• All grow closer to God and mature in the real basis and the greatest challenge for all missions, love.

"Though I speak with the tongues of men and of angels, and have not [love], I am become as sounding brass, or a tinkling cymbal. And though I have the gift of prophecy, and understand all mysteries, and all knowledge; and though I have all faith, so that I could remove mountains, and have not [love], I am nothing. And though I bestow all my goods to feed the poor, and though I give my body to be burned, and have not [love], it profiteth me nothing. [Love] suffereth long, and is kind; [love] envieth not; [love] vaunteth not itself, is not puffed up, Doth not behave itself unseemly, seeketh not her own, is not easily provoked, thinketh no evil; Rejoiceth not in iniquity, but rejoiceth in the truth; Beareth all things, believeth all things, hopeth all things, endureth all things. [Love] never faileth: but whether there be prophecies, they shall fail; whether there be tongues, they shall cease; whether there be knowledge, it shall vanish away. For we know in part, and we prophesy in part. But when that which is perfect is come, then that which is in part shall be done away. When I was a child, I spake as a child, I understood as a child, I thought as a child; but when I became a man, I put away childish things. For now we see through a glass, darkly; but then face to face: now I know in part; but then shall I know even as also I am known. And now abideth faith, hope, [love], these three; but the greatest of these is [love]" (1 Cor. 13).

The love of God is the most appropriate reflection we could have during any sunset. But genuine love will also produce actions on our part. Jesus said, "If you love me, keep my commandments" (John 14:15).

Reflect and respond as God guides.

9
Neighbors Along the Road

Several years ago, while en route to another city, a traveler was mugged, stripped of all his clothes, beaten, and left for dead beside the road. While he lay there suffering, a preacher happened by. For whatever reason, he chose to ignore the wounded man. Sometime later a deacon also passed that way. But he too kept going without offering to help.

Eventually a Christian layman saw the injured man, felt pity for him, applied first aid, and then carried him to a hotel where both the cost of that night's lodging and the time spent there until his recovery were paid for by the one whom Jesus used as a good example of a true "neighbor." (See Luke 10:30-36.)

People who experience misfortune in today's inner cities are still being helped through the combined efforts of both Christians and their secular neighbors who offer specialized services. Baptist Center Director Gladys Farmer greatly appreciates the wonderful spirit of cooperation among the many fine workers in the human service agencies throughout Montgomery. "Practically everyone shows genuine concern for the people they try to help," she says. And they, too, appreciate and encourage the work of the Baptist Center.

Society is now experiencing a change of seasons. On one side of the fence in the sixties, some tried to solve the problems of the poor with a "social gospel" that was all "social" and no "gospel." This is like performing the motions of farming without planting the seed.

On the other hand, some churches planted the gospel but practiced antisocial behavior toward those who needed them the most. This is like planting the seed and then letting it die from lack of water or soil nutrition.

Consequently, drastic results have affected both sides of the fence. School officials beg for stronger discipline to begin at home. Public health problems swell as morality declines. And prisons overflow because more and more citizens lack sufficient character training and self-discipline.

The church was once considered as the community's moral leaven. But more and more people outside its walls unashamedly say, "I can live all right without it." And too many inside avoid sharing eternal truths among the lost in neighborhoods where Jesus would probably have gone first.

Now the pendulum swings. Our secular neighbors are begging the church to motivate people to live by God's laws. And the church is realizing that "Go ye therefore, and teach all nations" (Matt. 28:19) includes loving everyone through missions at home. So now in a spirit of cooperation, neighbors from both sides of the fence are doing what they can to make the world a better place to live for everyone up and down the road.

Requests and Resources

Much too often churches consider only the spiritual aspect of a person's life and overlook the physical. On the other hand, secular agencies often consider only the physical needs and overlook the spiritual. Yet in reality, physical and spiritual needs often intertwine so much that proper ministry requires help for both needs at the same time.

A despondent person shivering in the cold, suffering from hunger pains would listen to words of love from someone handing them a coat and a hot meal much sooner than they would believe someone who offered them only words.

Actions demonstrate the feeling behind our words.

In fact, the Bible teaches that the genuineness of faith is proven through our actions toward those who are less fortunate. James 2:14-17 says, "My brothers, what good is it for someone to say that he has faith if his actions do not prove it? Can that faith save him? Suppose there are brothers or sisters who need clothes and don't have enough to eat. What good is there in your saying to them, 'God bless you! Keep warm and eat well!'—if you don't give them the necessities of life? So it is with faith: if it is alone and includes no actions, then it is dead" (TEV).

Yet food and clothes are only two of the many types of requests that come to the door and over the Baptist Center phone. A few requests that have involved the help of our secular neighbors include the following:

"Please help me find a downstairs apartment. I'm getting too feeble to climb these stairs any more."

"I was given away before I was a week old and have no birth certificate. I don't even know my real parents' name. Please help me straighten this out so my pension can begin."

"We were en route from Florida to Tennessee when our car broke down. Now we're stranded for more days than we have money. Can you help us?"

"I'm out of work. Do you know anybody needing a brick mason?"

"I know I need to quit drinking, and I try. But somehow it's got too much of a hold on me."

"I need a doctor, but I can't afford to go. I couldn't get even a prescription filled right now."

Help is available for all these needs, but sometimes a phone call is required to one of the secular agencies that many people don't even know exist.

Christians need to get acquainted with their neighbors

along the road because indigent victims of tragedy often need the church *plus* other types of help. Health clinics, nursing homes, special schools and rehabilitation centers, traveler's aid, homes for delinquent or neglected children, centers for alcoholism and other drug abuse, the Red Cross, Salvation Army, Faith Rescue Mission, employment offices, professional counselors, the police and court system, the county Department of Pensions and Security, the Veteran's Administration, and Social Security all offer a wide variety of services that might meet a desperate need in the life of someone we're trying to help.

These agencies know what the Baptist Center has to offer, and that simplifies their choosing from among many churches of many different denominations to ask help with a need some churches might not be prepared to handle. And Missionary Gladys Farmer appreciates the introduction to people she might never have met without some agency's referral.

"Referral" at the Baptist Center certainly doesn't mean dismissal. It means *cooperation* because the person being helped is always encouraged to return to take advantage of the first priority of the Baptist Center—Bible teaching. We believe that God's Word improves daily living as well as influences eternal destinies.

To Promote Prevention

Police Chief Charles Swindall says, "After working twenty-six years in the field of crime prevention I still scratch my head looking for solutions; but the answer remains the same—*Strong character teaching* and *instilling morality early in life for all citizens is the only thing that will decrease crime and make our city a safer place to live.* Without strength of character both the individual and the society in which he lives suffer.

"Everybody wants to decrease taxes, but *prevention* is the place to start. Most folks don't realize that every time a person goes to jail, it has already cost the taxpayer something to catch him and to defend him with a trial if he can't afford a lawyer. Then add any harm inflicted on innocent victims. Plus the support of his family while he's away in prison.

"Some estimates say it costs the state at least six thousand dollars a year for each person in prison. But for every crime committed, untold physical and emotional damage may be felt for several generations to come.

"It's impossible to compute the total cost of even one crime. But if you could, that would tell you just one benefit a community receives from character teaching in the lives of its residents.

"Time has proven that the further away people get from living by the Bible, the more crimes we experience and the more the cost to society in economic terms as well as overall well-being.

"Our police force appreciates the efforts of the Baptist Center and the local churches in teaching these character values. If we could get the millions of Christians interested enough in their community to teach at the grass-roots level and insist on better laws—nobody knows how much crime could be forestalled."

On Sunday, August 5, 1979, the *Montgomery Advertiser* headlines read, "City Has Decreased in Reported Crimes." We who are involved in inner-city ministry believe God had a part in lowering this crime rate—especially since we have been above the national average per capita.

Thanks to the wonderful cooperation of the Montgomery Housing Authority, the Baptist Center provides Bible-based character teaching to people of all ages in many different low-rent neighborhoods throughout the year. J. C. Miller, executive director of the Montgomery Housing Authority, made the following statement:

"I feel that Miss Gladys Farmer and inner-city missions

are answers to prayer as far as it pertains to the housing authority projects. At the time she came to our city several of our staff members were praying for such a ministry to be made available within the boundaries of the Housing Authority communities. There are many of us who know that the answer to all of our problems is to have a personal relationship with Jesus the Christ.

"It was not long after Miss Farmer came on the scene and began her visits with the volunteers that you could feel and sense a different attitude among many of our residents. There was even a decrease in acts of vandalism and other incidents of crime. Besides the spiritual aspect, we definitely feel that by an increase of missions of this sort, this could eventually lead to a savings to the taxpayer.

"Miss Gladys Farmer is a blessing to know because she radiates love wherever she goes. I have heard many small children call her 'Miss Bible Lady.' It is a wonder to behold, to look out in the project and see little groups of children sitting around a youth sharing the good news about Jesus. In my opinion, these little sessions are often the only time these little children even hear about a Savior being born for us all.

"One of my wishes and continued prayers is that this type of mission could be even broadened to include communities such as ours throughout the entire state of Alabama. We request your prayers as we will pray and thank our God for dedicated Christians like Miss Farmer and others who serve their Lord through the Baptist inner-city mission of Montgomery."

Missions in Rehabilitation

The Baptist Center and District Attorney Jimmy Evans both agree that rehabilitation starts with concern for the individual.

Concerned about the overcrowded prisons and an ever-spiraling rate of crime, District Attorney Evans boldly pioneered a nonprosecuting deferral program for eligible first offenders of petty larceny in the hope of rehabilitating them within the community instead of behind bars, if the offended party will also agree to this rehabilitating form of punishment.

In order to become eligible:

1. They must take certain tests that reveal their potential for rehabilitation or possible tendencies for worse crimes.

2. They must have returned the merchandise they stole and not have inflicted any bodily harm at the time of their crime.

3. They must come for counseling once a week for the length of their sentence with one of the district attorney's assistants. No more than one hundred are on this program at any given time.

4. They must attend school full-time if they're not working and part-time if they have a job.

5. They must contribute eight to ten hours a week in community service. This might be helping in Boy Scouts, a hospital or nursing home, or anywhere that will allow them to give time as volunteers. This makes them more caring persons, helps others, and builds the feeling of accomplishing something really worthwhile through service to others.

Other detailed requirements might also be added according to the special needs of the individual offender.

The testing of one boy who had stolen a pair of shoes revealed that even though he was in the ninth grade he could read only on a first grade, seventh month level. So as part of his deferral program, they required him to receive tutoring from a teacher trained in the Laubach method of teaching adult nonreaders.

About the time this case was being considered, the district attorney heard that the Baptist Center was training a group of volunteers to teach by the Laubach method. So he called to see if someone would be interested in teaching the young teenager to read.

Mr. Henry Fuqua agreed and met with the boy in one of the classrooms at Eastern Hills Church for many months. The youth progressed steadily and was proud of his new ability. One time he surprised Mr. Fuqua by saying, "I'm glad I got caught. I might've never learned to read without it."

"Do you read the funny papers and other things outside class?" Mr. Fuqua asked.

"Sure. I read everything I see," the youth answered, beaming from ear to ear.

These sessions went on for several months, and Mr. Fuqua always made good reports on the boy to the district attorney. But then, just a couple of months before finishing the required time for his deferral program, the boy rebelled against the unhappy home environment in which he lived and left town. Unfortunately, this violated his legal requirements and the court had to make stiffer demands.

These unfortunate results cast no reflection on the congenial cooperation between the district attorney and the Baptist Center because they encourage the work of each other wholeheartedly. They only show that every endeavor of helping people includes many hidden facets of concern that must be worked through.

We pray that God will continue to multiply the seed that was planted in this young boy's life so it will result in even more growth further down the road.

Chaplain Elmer Neilson says, "Ministry in Tutwiler Prison influenced the atmosphere so much that other institutions started asking how they could have the same thing." He was referring to the effects of the weekly visits by Rev. Milton Boyd and volunteers from Westside Mission and First Baptist Church.

So many in correctional institutions desperately need

someone who will listen to them talk. As a state employee, Chaplain Neilson's job involves walking among the women at Tutwiler and, at a different time, among the boys at Frank Lee Youth Center so that they can share their feelings with someone who really cares. But only one chaplain among so many leaves room for the help of others too.

Sometimes a different person or women talking to women adds a new dimension to their thinking; and Brother Boyd's messages always give them real strength from God's Word. Because he's black they also listen better.

So many Baptist men have developed an interest in this work that the Baptist Center conducted intensive training sessions to prepare them for this specialized ministry. Six nearby correctional institutions now have a Baptist witness, and the wardens always thank them for coming. Many of the prisoners say it gives them strength to face each day, and several have made genuine commitments to Jesus Christ.

Chaplain Neilson requests your prayers for these spiritual babes who face tests of their faith that few people outside fully comprehend. "But even more," he adds, "if only people would let Christ take first place in their lives before sin caused them to go so far . . . "

We've got to lift the poor lost humanity up now or expect them to pull us down. They're not going to come to us; we'll have to go to them. And that's what Christian social ministry is all about—the church working within the world as missionaries to people with unmet needs.

Other Churches as Neighbors

Occasionally we hear comments such as, "Why should the Baptist Center go into different communities to teach the poor when they have a little church of some denomination nearby?"

The Baptist Center is an effort of home missions to minister to areas with an abundance of unmet needs, both physical and spiritual. When physical needs overwhelm a person's ability to comprehend spiritual truths, he often requires a *different* kind of ministry than the average church offers on Sunday.

In fact, some people would not feel comfortable in just any local church because others might stare at their obvious need for better clothes, shoes, or dental work. Some people do look different, talk different, and act different; but all people have the same feelings and the same need for Jesus Christ. Such discomfort prevents them from ever going back if they were not made to feel welcome. Unfortunately, some church policies or unspoken prejudice actually discourage some from worship attendance at all.

But the churches where they fit in physically often do not offer them as much spiritually. Many churches have very small Sunday Schools or none at all. Their pastors frequently hold more than one job and cannot visit the people during the week to discover their unmet needs as they wish they could.

Dr. J. R. White, pastor of Montgomery's First Baptist Church, said, "The Baptist Center is the best way to minister to the needs of the people we haven't been able to reach. We have to face the fact that some people just wouldn't feel comfortable coming to First Baptist, even though most of our congregation would try very hard to make them feel welcome. So if they won't come to us, we should take Christ to them through active missions.

"The concern of our church is reflected in the abundance of our people who have helped as volunteers in every area of the Baptist Center ministry and now even sponsor the worship service and children's classes there on Sunday.

"First Baptist has supported this work from the very beginning and is thrilled with all it has done for our city. We look forward to the growth of the new areas of ministry that help us find even more ways we can minister to people in the name of Christ."

Teamwork Tokens

"Long distance calling Miss Gladys Farmer," the voice on the telephone said.

In a voice of cautious surprise the missionary replied, "This is she."

Then she was informed of the death of the Lebanese lady whom the Baptist Center had helped so much while she lived in Montgomery. Several months ago the lady's arteries had hardened to such an extent that she needed the kind of round-the-clock medical attention that could only be found in the state mental hospital. Several neighbors along the road had initially assisted her in securing this help. And now someone was calling to ask what they should do concerning her burial arrangements.

Miss Farmer took a minute before she replied. Even when those we love are old in years, death both shocks and saddens us. Across the missionary's mind flashed the visit just a few weeks ago when she and several Baptist Center volunteers who had grown very close to the Lebanese lady traveled to Tuscaloosa to give her a special birthday party. She had been very happy that they cared enough to come so far. Other patients and nurses said that the visit brightened their day as well.

But now the caller said he could find no relative to claim the body, and he wanted to ask the Baptist Center what to do.

"Can you wait until I make some more phone calls, please?" the missionary asked. After he agreed to await her call, Miss Farmer got prayerfully busy making many necessary calls. She recalled how the lady had said her parents had raised her in the Catholic faith. So Miss Farmer called to request a burial plot beside some other deceased members of her family in a Catholic cemetery. They graciously agreed.

Then she called the White Chapel Funeral Home to see

what a casket and shroud would cost. As she relayed the woman's name the spokesman for the funeral home said, "I know that lady. We bought the land for this building from her. Even after her original home was torn down and these facilities were built, she frequently visited the grounds to walk among the trees and flowers she loved.

"You don't have to worry about her funeral arrangements. We'll send a hearse to bring her back from Tuscaloosa and give her a casket and clothes for a decent burial."

Those who attended the Lebanese lady's memorial services consisted primarily of Christians who came to know her through the Baptist Center and others who had helped as concerned neighbors.

Caring for the dead is soon done and not too hard. But caring for the living always comes with a cry for urgency, always promising massive tangles of problems and never guaranteeing progress that one might see. But we trust that "God's Word shall not return void" (see Isa. 55:11).

Off and on throughout the day the Baptist Center and their secular neighbors constantly cooperate in meeting people's needs. Traveler's Aid might send a transient over for a plate of food before they give him a bus ticket to a city where he's already been promised work. The Cadet Center might bring one they've been treating for alcoholism there to get a pair of shoes. Social workers from various public agencies often ask the Baptist Center to help gather clothes for a family whose home has just burned. Recently there came a call for someone to provide lodging in their home and transportation for the mother of a young serviceman from another city who was flown to Baptist Hospital for special care.

The county health department treats many indigent patients, but sometimes someone from the Baptist Center provided their transportation to the clinic. The Baptist Center does not have sleeping accommodations, but the Salvation

Army and Faith Rescue Mission have always been very cooperative in accepting their referrals. Miss Farmer has spent countless hours late at night completing reports on mental patients and parolees that other agencies needed concerning those people.

The Gideons have voluntarily brought Bibles several times. The Jaycees and Kiwanis Clubs have taken children from the Baptist Center on several shopping sprees and recreational outings.

When a Baptist Center freezer had problems too expensive to fix, Miss Farmer gave it to Goodwill; and they in turn fixed a needy person's wheelchair. A sack of groceries and words of encouragement often help to tide a person over when he is waiting to be processed by the Food Stamp Program or the employment service; and Miss Farmer rejoices with him when those needs are met. Doctors and hospitals might never know that a person has had contact with the Baptist Center, but on many occasions it took a lot of tactful encouragement to get someone to finally go before the problem grew more difficult to treat. And who can measure the value of a changed attitude by someone who now says, "I'm not afraid to die" or of a shut-in who can now be cheerful instead of depressed?

In asking teachers through the Baptist Center what progress they can observe in a work so well known for its hardness, one said, "It might not seem like much to some people, but when I started seeing the ladies in my class grow in patience and begin sharing and helping each other, I knew we were making a little progress."

Another teacher of children told about a little girl named Karen who even at the age of five was mean to other children. She would hit or kick another child for no obvious reason. Nothing anyone could say or do changed her actions.

But the teacher made it a point to give her a lot of attention and hugged her when it seemed appropriate. Finally after about two years the children were lining up to go somewhere and Karen accidentally tripped another classmate. Much to their surprise she took the fallen boy by the arm, lifted him up, and said, "I'm so sorry. Please excuse me."

Every child in the group stared at her as though they thought the words came from outer space. But the days that followed proved that Karen really was changing because she had now received the love of God in her life.

And that's what makes mission efforts all worthwhile. The emotions, the exertion of efforts, and the exhaustion surely test one's commitment. But the joys far outweigh the hardships. And each soul sheltered in the love of God makes service a small price to pay and witnessing a privilege beyond words.

Dear, Jesus: I am a child
I Love you Nobody can't change
my life like you can't I am glad
your my God father, And my Friend
I will always remember you If
I come where you are at.

Miss Farmer found this prayer while cleaning a classroom in the Baptist Center. This makes it all worthwhile!

Appendix

A number of practical resources have been developed to help churches begin some of the kind of ministries carried out by the Baptist Center in Montgomery, Alabama.

Woman's Missionary Union publishes the following Mission Action Group Guides which can be purchased individually:

- The Aging
- Alcohol and Drug Abusers
- Child Care
- Disaster Relief
- Headliners
- Internationals
- Juvenile Rehabilitation
- Language Groups
- Military
- Nonreaders
- Prisoner Rehabilitation
- Resort Areas
- The Sick

For further information about these guides, write:

Woman's Missionary Union
600 North 20th Street
Birmingham, Alabama 35203

The Baptist General Convention of Texas has a *How to Begin Series*. Included in this package are the following helps:

- A Church Community Weekday Ministry Survey
- The Church Senior Adult Club Program
- The Church Community Ministry to International Families
- The Church Community Tutoring Program
- The Church Community Mother's Day Off Program

- The Church Community Telephone Reassurance Ministry
- The Church Day Care Ministry
- The Church Holiday Hospitality House Program
- The Senior Adult Transportation Ministry
- The Church Community Club Program
- The Church Community Clinic Program

In addition to the materials in this package, Texas Baptists publish *Church Child Care/Day Care Curriculum Planning Guide.*

For information about these materials, write:

> The Baptist General Convention of Texas
> 307 Baptist Building
> Dallas, Texas 75201

The Home Mission Board of the Southern Baptist Convention publishes the following materials:

- *Aging, Senior Impact: Handbook on Aging and Senior Adult Ministries* by Tom E. Prevost
- *Volunteers in Christian Social Ministries* by Edward B. Freeman, Jr. and Judith E. Freeman
- *Love with No Strings*
- *Handbook on Literacy Missions*

In addition to these resources, the Home Mission Board offers a number of pamphlets without cost:

- Church-Community Weekday Ministries
- Christian Social Ministries
- Literacy Missions

For further information about these materials, write:

> Home Mission Board, SBC
> 1350 Spring Street, N.W.
> Atlanta, Georgia 30309

Date Due